THE WEIGHT OF EMPTINESS

COMFORT AND HOPE FOR THE LOSS OF A LOVED ONE

Patricia Elliot

AuthorHouse™ UK
1663 Liberty Drive
Bloomington, IN 47403 USA
www.authorhouse.co.uk
Phone: 0800.197.4150

Published by AuthorHouse 08/12/2020

ISBN: 978-1-7283-5192-6 (sc)
ISBN: 978-1-7283-5191-9 (e)

Library of Congress Control Number: 2020913572

Print information available on the last page.

*Any people depicted in stock imagery provided by Getty Images are models,
and such images are being used for illustrative purposes only.
Certain stock imagery © Getty Images.*

This book is printed on acid-free paper.

authorHOUSE®

Collage of Bruce's life

This book is for you, my beautiful boy. In your own words you were '.......*trapped in another character.....*'. You had many aspects to your character, the *'dark'* and the *'light'* just like the weight of emptiness in my heart which is dark and heavy, often too heavy to bear. I find myself sobbing uncontrollably but then I remember that you are free from pain and the weight becomes *'light'* and laughter returns when I think of your smile, creativity and wonderful memories. The words adapted from the song (by Johnny Nash[1]) played at the celebration of your life say it all:

'I can see clearly now the rain has gone, all of the bad feelings have disappeared......'

From Bruce's pain I found more courage and resilience than I believed possible but these gave me the ability to endure every day. Patricia Elliot

---

[1]   Nash, Johnny *I can see clearly now (excerpt)* released 1972 Album *I can see clearly now*

About the Author

Patricia knew from an early age that she would write a book one day. Now, years later she has written numerous academic books and is now writing this second personal book, the first being '7 Attributes for Success (Inner Success and Happiness)[2]. You can find out more on Patricia's website www.mindcircles.co.uk and social media sites. Patricia is currently also writing *The Secret of Courage and Resilience*[3] the sequel to *7 Attributes for Success.*

Having lost her gorgeous son Bruce to suicide over five years ago she realised that there was a need for a book where she could share her experience of such a trauma while also helping people who have been affected by suicide realise that they are not alone. She sincerely hopes that this book will offer comfort and hope to many and that a loved one should be remembered so that their life was not lived in vain. She has felt guilt that it has taken her so long to write but also realised her need to grieve *and* find the right words for sharing such a personal experience of loss.

Her vision for all her personal books is to empower and improve the lives of every individual so that they realise their true potential through courage and resilience. After sharing the suicide of her son on social media she was contacted by many people with similar experiences and it became clear that this book was much needed.

However, it has not been easy writing this book, it was the most daunting as Patricia has opened her heart to what has been the most challenging experience of her life. Much as she desperately would love to have Bruce back in her life, she knows he is at peace. Patricia has been overwhelmed by the sharing of stories from people who have suffered loss of a loved one and that they have felt comfortable enough to share these stories with her. She is privileged and honoured to include them in this book. Patricia believes and knows that sharing is caring and helps healing. Patricia hopes that people will continue to share and feel comfortable enough to contact her through her website.

---

[2]   Elliot, Patricia (2010) *7 Attributes for Success (Inner Success and Happiness)* Authorhouse and available on Amazon and www.mindcircles.co.uk website

[3]   Elliot, Patricia (2020) *The Secret of Courage and Resilience* Authorhouse and available on Amazon and www.mindcircles.co.uk

I have so many people to thank for helping me throughout my life, both in the happy and not so happy times. There are too many to mention here but I must thank those few who have gone the 'extra mile' particularly in my times of need.

A huge thanks to all my friends and colleagues who provided suggestions for the title of my book. I finally decided on the title *'The Weight of Emptiness'* suggested by Zena Von-Rollock and I am forever grateful and honoured to use it.

A massive thank you to Chris Gair, my neighbour who came with me that fateful night and was the one to go into my son's flat. I am forever grateful to Chris for sparing me the tragic scene. I don't think I would ever have been able to erase that scene from my memory.

I thank and praise the police who attended the scene that night. They were efficient, compassionate and courteous. It was a comfort to me that Bruce's brother knew one of the police detectives attending that night.

I express gratitude to Cameron Duncan of Adams and Duncan[4], Funeral Directors, for his compassion and understanding at such a difficult, tragic time. From the moment of first contact, Cameron was sympathetic and respectful. He gave a personal and professional service and I could not have asked for more. It was just what my son, Bruce, would have wanted.

My thanks go to Jane Patmore[5], Celebrant who honoured the character and talents of Bruce in a moving and emotional tribute (Appendix II) at the Celebration of Bruce's life.

I thank all those who sent messages of condolence: his good friend Mette, his friends Karen Welsh (now Elliott), Michelle Lundie and others from Cleveden Secondary who remembered him fondly, his friend Edward Davis (aka *'Wood'*), Markus Olesen (Sweden) who told me, *'....we had a very strong and special friendship ....and many memories........spending many endless nights together.........we were very comfortable with each other's company.....',* everyone at The Westbourne Tavern, London, all friends in London, Denmark, LA and Cuba to mention but a few.

Dez Clarke shared the story of his loss of Bruce, a true friend and mate (Appendix IV) but also sent a message which describes *'The Bruce'* as he was affectionately known. Excerpts from this message

---

[4]   Adams and Duncan, Funeral Directors www.adamsandduncan.co.uk
[5]   Jane Patmore, Celebrant http://www.yourserviceinscotland.co.uk/

shows how Bruce appeared to the outside world, yet somehow sadly never realised it himself! He never boasted, was always modest (too modest perhaps) and just thought of himself as being *'him'*.

'The Bruce'

'I have soooo very many lovely and funny stories of mine, ours, Bruce's escapades in London and LA as well as our quieter times just talking on our own. I really connected with Bruce... .....when Bruce was living in Venice Beach he joined the little UK gang, going to parties, hitting the beaches..............he got work in Hollywood at events and as assistant to a Hollywood photographer...............for every few moments of sadness I have thinking of Bruce and how dark a place he must have been in to decide to leave us all I'm strangely overwhelmed with huge smiles and belly laughter remembering times with him and his HUGELY FUN CHARACTER........ Bruce is a massive part of all our lives down here, both the work team and the London scene..... what a wonderfully fun guy to have at every occasion........incredibly creative and without fear – always chasing an adventure...........a super enthusiastically infectious, handsome, charismatic, charming, eloquently spoke and always dapperly dressed young Scottish Man..........

He was sooooooo very popular with the ladies (I hope you are proud to hear)..............*When watching a Hollywood Rom-Com recently I found myself in tears not at the movie but at seeing the leading actress who was a girlfriend of Bruce while we worked in LA...............yes! I was definitely envious of his suave and charismatic, confident, smooth skills not just with the ladies but everyone he came to be in the company of...................none of us are perfect and Bruce wasn't either....he was troubled as we all can be but he so made up for it in such other wonderful ways ....I cannot express in this short message just how very much I will miss him xxx'* Dez, a true friend and mate. I included some of this beautiful message in my tribute (Appendix III) to Bruce on the day of the Celebration of his life.

I thank everyone who shared stories of their loss (Appendix IV). I feel honoured and privileged to include them in this book.

I am forever grateful to *'Mabozza'* who managed to extract the thousands of photographs from Bruce's many hard drives and back-ups: no mean feat as I know Bruce backed up everything more than once and with different passwords!!

Thanks to the amazing photographer, Sonja Blietschau[6] for her assistance in selecting and preparing photographs of Bruce and those made by him (Appendix VII) in the required format for insertion in this book. Sonja had never met Bruce but after time spent going through his many photographs and personal belongings she shared that she felt as if she not only knew my son but understood him. I hope that by including photographs in this book that you, the reader, will feel that in some small way you know and understand Bruce too.

I had many people to thank when I wrote *7 Attributes for Success* and I continue to give thanks as they supported me when I was hit by the tragedy — the suicide of my first-born son, Bruce.

---

[6]   Sonja Blietschau Photography www.sonjab-photography.com

Bruce often talked about his friend and mentor, the professional photographer Martin Gilfeather[7]. I thank him for being there for Bruce and express my heartfelt gratitude for his comforting words when describing Bruce: *'there was a remarkable dignity about Bruce...he was a good man'*.

Those who have read my '*7 Attributes*' book will know I talk about courage and resilience. Now I believe that I have courage and resilience in abundance, but these have been tested to their limits after my tragic loss.

I wanted to write a book about my loss and I beat myself up for not having written it sooner. However, the time must be right; loss and grief are complicated and extraordinary and sometimes you feel fine and other times you just go to pieces!

I sincerely hope that this book will help all those who have lost a loved one, especially a child (no matter the circumstances) as well as those who are living with the fear that their child might commit suicide.

As always, I can rely on my close friend (more like family) Margaret Robinson to make me cups of tea, take me out for dinner and just being there as a listener. Another close friend Morfydd continues to offer emotional support with weekly tea and chats to keep me going. Despite living abroad my friends and colleagues Stuart Mallinson and his wife Anne continue to be positive motivators.

My thanks and gratitude to Peter Batty who edited my manuscript with the utmost care and understanding, honing my thoughts and adding clarity. This was a particularly daunting task since I tend to re-write when I review chapters or pages. With Peter's changes I can truly say 'enough is enough'!

My friend Bill Winn is also there to support me throughout the difficult periods of my life.

Sadly, the size of the book does not permit me to mention all those who supported and continue to support me, but you know who you are and whoever and wherever you are I thank you from the bottom of my heart.

Like Bruce, my head is always so full of ideas that sometimes it feels as if it could burst. Also, like Bruce I am a perfectionist and worry that my book will not be perfect, but it is written from the heart. I must also thank my good friend and colleague Walter Taylor for his never-ending patience, putting up with me for years and being always ready to make changes almost at 'my beck and call' whether developing MindCircles[8] or my online Steps for Success program. I can hear Walter's voice: *'just publish it!'* I also thank Walter for designing the covers for this book.

I could not do without the talent and skills of Eddie Macarthur of Stealth Studios who keeps me 'smiling' when developing my MindBites[9] meditations.

The Weight of Emptiness is written in memory of my gorgeous son Bruce who just could not and did not want to cope with the way the world was going. In his own words he felt "....*trapped in another*

---

[7]   Martin Gilfeather, professional photographer
[8]   MindCircles www.mindcircles.co.uk
[9]   MindBites – video and audio meditations available on www.mindcircles.co.uk or www.stepsforsuccess.co.uk

character….". He was so creative throughout his life, being involved with sculpting, acting, art, writing and photography and he suggested many tips and tools for my *7 Attributes* book to help people realise their true potential. Despite giving me these very helpful, positive suggestions, he just could not overcome the many challenges he had faced in his life.

The world has lost a wonderfully creative, talented actor, writer and photographer with a genius eye and ability to tell a story through his photography but more than this I have lost my gorgeous 'boy'.

Although it is over 5 years since Bruce committed suicide it can seem like yesterday. I shared my loss with many people, through my blogs (excerpts in Appendix VI) and also on social media because I realised that many who suffer from depression or have feelings of suicide or decide to commit suicide are high functioning individuals who, to the outside world, do not appear depressed or even 'low'. Indeed, they can seem extraordinarily happy and excited. I know that for Bruce it was his highly creative and over analytical mind that excited him and enthralled me as well as those around him. However, what he could not 'let go of' was his drive for perfection even when told by others that 'it' was perfect.

To me he was perfect and I thank you, Bruce, for being in my life.

Please tell your loved ones often that you love them. You never know when you might lose them.

> *Have the courage and resilience to live life to the fullest. Remember sharing helps healing.*

Contents

Bruce: Thoughtful sitting

Everyone you meet is fighting a battle you know nothing about. Be kind always. Robin Williams[10]

My mind was racing:

What made me think something was wrong?
Why did I delay in taking any action?
Would it have made a difference?

When I did act, I had this dreadful knot in my stomach. I prayed everything would be alright.

I went to Bruce's flat with my neighbour and friend, Chris Gair. We did not need to break down the door. It was slightly open. I moved to go in, but Chris held me back and he went in. I heard his voice calling 'Bruce, Bruce'. Time seemed to stop. I was desperate for Chris to come out with Bruce beside him. But he came out alone. I heard words, as if in the far distance *'He's gone, Pat, He's gone'*.

I wanted to rush in, comfort my boy, but Chris stopped me. I started to say something but was interrupted by Chris' words which were to bring comfort later *'He looks peaceful, he looks peaceful'*. I cannot thank

---

[10]   Williams, Robin McLaurin (dob 21/07/1951 to dod 11/08/2014) – actor who paraphrased the quote said to be attributed to Ian Maclaren, the pen name of Dr John Watson (3/11/1850 to 6/05/1907)

Chris enough for what he did for me that terrible night and especially for sparing me the tragic scene which I know I could never have erased from my mind. At least my memory of Bruce remains as my boy: the complex *'dark'* and *'light'* character that he was.

You never know how you are going to act or react when faced with the awful tragedy that your son has committed suicide.

Time stands still, yet it rushes on for the outside world. The police needed to be called. Neighbours started appearing. I hear myself saying: *My son has committed suicide.*

I find myself telling everyone I meet, neighbours, strangers, everyone: *'My son has committed suicide'.* I'm not sure why, perhaps it was my way of dealing with the news, somehow to make it real.

Over 5 years have passed since Bruce committed suicide and the pain is as raw today as it was then. Yet how I feel changes from day to day and even minute to minute. I know people will empathise with this. Grief feels like the sea. It can be calm and just lap around me then suddenly it hits me like a thunderous crashing wave when I least expect it. The weight is heavy and all-consuming. It can feel so heavy, not just sitting in my stomach but weighing my shoulders down so much that I can't breathe and feel as if I am drowning. At these fleeting moments I wish it was so and I could be with him but these moments pass, and I know that I must live. He would want that and I want to share my experience so that Bruce's life is not in vain.

Experiencing the ever-changing weight of grief and the empty space left in my heart are the reasons I chose the title of this book, *The Weight of Emptiness.*

Immediately after this traumatic event I openly shared my experience on social media. At first this was not met well by his siblings but when I told them about the reluctance to talk about suicide they realised that sharing would help others. This has proved to be the case as many people contacted me with words of support, encouragement and some to share their experience. I share some stories at the end of this book.

Sharing helps healing.

When a death occurs, whether in traumatic circumstances or not, there are many practical matters to attend to. These practicalities can generate friction and anger, often creating a rift among family members or they can bring people together. My heartfelt thanks again to Cameron Duncan of Adams and Duncan funeral directors for their kindness at such a difficult, emotional time.

In the case of suicide there must be a post-mortem and I talk later in the book about attending the morgue. I also discuss what happens, what to expect, what emotions I experienced in the hope that this brings comfort to others who may have to face similar situations. I include some humour or should I say black humour moments as I know Bruce would appreciate these.

I did not want to rush into having a 'funeral' or what I prefer to call the celebration of Bruce's life. Partly this was due to trying to find all his friends so that they could be invited. This may sound simple but most people, especially young people, do not have address books, and you need to turn to social media networks for information! This is where my sharing on Facebook and other social media sites helped and I was able to contact many people who then managed to come along to the celebration.

I discuss the celebration of Bruce's life later in the book and how having this and the gathering afterwards went a long way in bringing comfort to me, knowing how many people valued having Bruce in their life. Nonetheless I know that without exception they would all rather have him present in their lives now.

I discuss in detail throughout the chapters what it is like to cope (or not) on some or many days. I know everyone who suffers the loss of a loved one will grieve differently. They say there are five stages of grief and I talk about these in some detail later. Indeed a few years ago I wrote about grief but since losing Bruce my thoughts on the five stages have changed dramatically.

Grief may have five stages, but these stages do not always happen in a neat sequence. They can occur all in one day: even almost one minute and sometimes all in one moment.

People who know of your loss, even close friends (and family) might or will avoid you. This is not because they are being rude, but more often because they don't know what to say. I try to make them comfortable by starting the conversation and letting them know that it is OK to talk about Bruce.

Grief can overwhelm you when you least expect it. In a supermarket, at a meeting, just walking along the street, listening to music. Something triggers and you find yourself sobbing uncontrollably.

Crying uncontrollably is good for you so try not to hold back. However, when it happens in public you might feel silly or people might try to ask you what is wrong which can make it worse. I have a technique that I use for such public circumstances and I refer to this as my *'Red door/Blue door'* technique described in Appendix V. I know it helps me (and it certainly helped when I spoke about Bruce at the celebration of his life).

'You handle your grief well' said my good friend, Liz. This comforts me as I know that she sees beneath my exterior. I am also glad that this is how I appear to others as I know Bruce would not want me to be unhappy.

I describe Bruce's letters—one to me (Appendix I) and one to each of his siblings. His letter to me was heartfelt, telling me that it was no-one's fault and that he just did not want to be here anymore. He said that he loved me dearly and told me that everything would be OK. His letter brought me some comfort. However, some have said that it must have brought closure, but I see his letter as helping me to think differently because I know I can't get Bruce back and live my old life. Instead, I can live in what is now a new way of life.

I am sure I am not alone in thinking *'what if...'*. So, I share my experience of reflecting on the past and perhaps what I might have changed. But as I tell everyone who is a parent, we do the best we can with the tools we have at the time.

Something else I describe are my thoughts on those that talk about me being a survivor. I don't like this word as it implies that I have triumphed over something which is in the past. However, my son's suicide is not and will never be in the past: it will be in my mind and heart forever. So, I prefer to see myself as enduring each moment of every day.

Bruce's suicide changed my life forever and I am enduring moments every day when going about my ordinary business, whether that is having a cuppa, shopping or just sitting!

I have always thought of myself as positive and resilient but Bruce's suicide has tested my resilience and continues to test me in ways I never thought possible. I know people mean well when they say time heals, but for me, time provides (and can give you too) the tools and techniques to endure the everyday moments.

Some people may say that they could have written this book and no doubt that is true. I would say go on, after all, it is often said that there is a book in everyone. However, writing any book is no mean feat and writing this one has been an emotional rollercoaster. I have been motivated by the many people, family, friends and colleagues who have supported me in the process.

The loss of Bruce has changed my life forever and I wanted to tell people how important it is to recognise your emotions and know how to cope with them, with the comfort of knowing that it is OK to let your emotions pour out in the moments that you feel you cannot go on.

Writing this book has been difficult as no two people experience the loss of a loved one in the same way. My hope is that by sharing my experience of losing my gorgeous son offers comfort and hope and helps those in similar situation realise that they are not alone.

There is so much information on talk being necessary—even the answer—to people with depression and suicidal thoughts. I know talking and sharing is necessary but I am not sure that it is the answer. This is because I describe in this book how Bruce was able to talk avidly on many subjects but not about his own emotions (although more than happy to talk about the psychological research on emotions!)

My son Bruce did talk to me sometimes about possibly being bi-polar and asked me why he had not been diagnosed. I really didn't know the answer! I told him that no-one thought about this all these years ago and I just thought that his behaviour was just about being a teenager.

Oh, how I wish I could turn the clock back. Sadly, this is not possible but if this book can help those who are worried then in some way it is doing its purpose and Bruce's life will not have been in vain.

I count myself fortunate because I can talk!

So, for me, talking openly about my son's suicide and about his life is what helped and continues to help me cope with my loss.

However, I do know that many people can find talking about their loss very difficult, but I recommend that you try; it does help. It raises emotions and that is good for you and helps the healing process. It is also good to let the tears flow.

Sadly, mental health and any talk surrounding it is or still seems to be for many people a 'no-go' area and carries a stigma.

Even before Bruce's death, I had personal experience of close friends suffering from depression and bi-polar disorder among others. I was horrified by the response of others when dealing with or speaking about those suffering from any mental health. Responses varied from ignoring that there was any problem to words such as 'they are mental', 'they need to get a life', 'they are psycho' and so on. I pointed out that if these individuals had been diagnosed with cancer or had broken their backs and were in wheelchairs most people would rally round and help where they could and not make light of the situation.

Much information on mental health refers to the importance of talking about mental health problems and of course if you do suffer from mental health issues you should consult an appropriate medical, psychiatric or psychological professional. The issue I have with talking about our mental health is that from my experience of Bruce (and possibly many people like him) he would not talk about his mental health, but he would and indeed did talk a great deal about physical health, nutrition and how eating well was good for your health.

Bruce did seek professional psychiatric help, but I realised from our many conversations that when meeting such professionals, he would talk at an academic level, seeking information on health but not actually talking about his own mental health.

There are many people out there who will neither talk nor share their thoughts, so I hope that this book can help families who find themselves with a loved one that does not want to talk!

Of course, please remember that loved ones who do suffer from any mental health problems need all the support they can get particularly from those close to them. So just be there. Try to persuade them to seek professional help too.

On my journey through life I have experienced many challenges, but nothing really prepared me for the suicide of my son. I draw from my own experiences in this book, but I may add that I am not super-human and have not always dealt with the life issues as positively as I should have.

I am fortunate to have a following of readers who remind me of my own tips and tools detailed in my *7 Attributes* book and for this I thank them and ask them to continue to remind me when 'I fall by the wayside'!

I am a perfectionist and find myself reading, re-writing and so on until I have to tell myself enough is enough. I don't mind if comments are constructive, but I also know that there will always be some people who like to criticise and bring you down. You must ignore these people and concentrate on those who want you to succeed.

I am fortunate that my confidence was given a boost when I was asked to write academic books and there is nothing better for confidence and your spirits when you receive comments such as 'well written, easy to read and understand'.

Writing the academic books was the catalyst for getting to grips with writing this book.

When I look back at my *7 Attributes* book I realise that Bruce (like many, even me at times) did possess the 7 Attributes but he was just not able to always use them successfully to see his way through life's challenges. I am still forever grateful to him for helping me understand that not everyone can cope and many of those who choose suicide at that moment just cannot see a way through.

This still does not make my loss any easier to bear. However, the music we played at the celebration of his life summed it up for Bruce.

> *I can see clearly now the rain has gone…..* from *I Can See Clearly Now,* a song originally recorded by Johnny Nash[11]

I make no excuse for repeating this. There will always be those like Bruce who just cannot talk or cope with life, but my hope is that talking about my son through my book will offer comfort to those who have lost a loved one, particularly to suicide, and give some comfort to those who are going through traumatic times.

By the time you are reading this I know you have bought my book. I sincerely hope that it helps you in some way and is there when you need it or just to read through. More than that I hope that the stories shared by those who have suffered the loss of a loved one will help too, even motivate and inspire you to think and act differently.

If it is at all possible please start looking at your life from a different, more positive perspective even in the face of trauma.

Before Bruce died I wrote about grief in its many forms. Like others who have written about grief and its various stages it is only after suffering this traumatic loss did I realise that writing about grief and the actual suffering of grief is so very different.

Grief can hit at any time and one stage or even all the stages of grief can happen in one day. It can be triggered by anything, even the mundane, such as buying something at the supermarket. You might find yourself suddenly overcome, tears flowing, even sobbing. My trigger is the song *'I Can See Clearly Now'* by Johnny Nash or any classical music and I find myself sobbing uncontrollably.

This is natural and you should not hold back your tears. The problem is that we don't want to do this in public for fear of embarrassment. I offer some of my techniques that I use when in public to stop this from happening or at least lessening the embarrassment.

---

[11]   *'I can see clearly now'* – original lyrics and music by Johnny Nash in an album by Johnny Nash titled I Can See Clearly Now

However, when you are alone you should let the tears flow. You should also try to find some time alone to do this. Recently I found myself sobbing uncontrollably but I let the tears flow. Doing this does bring some sense of relief. I am fortunate that I can do this. I am also able to talk about Bruce and this helps. However, there are many people who cannot bring themselves to talk about their lost loved one and for those it is important to seek professional help.

Grief, like life, is like an ocean. It is vast and uncontrollable. Grief also varies in weight. It can be a heavy burden to bear, too much for some people who may never smile, feel or be happy again. My sincere hope is that by reading my book these people will find a way back to at least smile or feel better some of the time. Later in the book I talk about the weight of grief and how it changes almost daily for me.

Remember that many things are thrown at you in life, much of which are outside of your control. Often you may think that you are helpless to do anything about these things, but you still have a choice as to how you deal with them. The choices can be good, bad, even terrible but you can decide what you do and how you face these challenging, sometimes tragic situations. Take a moment to consider the questions that follow.

Do you sink?

Do you swim with or against the tide or current?

Do you surf the waves?

Do you sail through?

Is your grief like a heavy stone round your neck, pulling you down?

Do you find the weight of this stone changes depending on how you feel, or what situation you are in?

Is the weight of your grief heaviest when it is triggered by something such as music, or art or a place or something else?

Think about these questions for a moment and ask yourself what you do to ease your pain or what you think you could do.

Tip: Although you cannot change the past you can change how you view the past and learn from it.

To do this can be frightening because you must also be honest with yourself and you might not like what you see. All I ask is that you are true to yourself. You also must take responsibility and accountability for your actions.

I have bad days, awful days, but also uplifting days. I say Bruce's name, I talk to him, I can feel him beside me, and this gives me comfort. Of course, I would love nothing more than to have him actually be with me but that is not possible. So, I try to look at the way he would want me to live and I am certain that he would not want me to be sad forever.

I let the tears flow (often) and then I think of something that he did that made me happy and I find myself laughing. Laughter helps me move forward another minute, hour and day.

> *Laughter is the best medicine and it helps me move forward another minute, hour and day.*

If I can touch the lives of some people in my writing, then it will all be worthwhile.

By sharing this dark experience of my tragic loss I hope to open your mind to the possibility that you can learn from the dark times and have the strength to go on even in the face of tragedy. Not everyone may be able to do this, but I know that for many people my experiences will resonate with them and they will be able to empathise with my experiences.

> *From our greatest challenges we (can and do) gain our greatest strength*

I know I will always have questions such as:

Could I have done more for Bruce when he was younger?

Life was not always easy for me and my four children and I find myself looking back and wondering if I could or should have done more. This makes me feel guilt and even shame[12] because I feel bad about not doing more for them. However, as I often tell others, there is no training to be a parent and we do the best we can with the knowledge and tools we have at the time.

> Remember: *Don't judge people: a smile does not mean that they have no problems or are not suffering. Nothing could be further from the truth.*

Indeed, very recently when coming home by plane, a flight attendant pulled my earphones and they caught on my earring which flew into the air and was lost.

This was precious to me as it was an 'Ashes into Glass'[13] earring containing the ashes of Bruce

---

12   Lewis, Helen Block (1971) *Shame and Guilt* International University Press, New York
13   Ashes into Glass – tribute jewellery using the ashes of a loved one www.ashesintoglass.co.uk

I was clearly upset and distraught, but with the earring being so small I realised quickly that it would probably not be found. Unfortunately, the flight attendants were not really interested in finding it and said that it would be up to the cleaners to find it but the earring was never found!

Rather than dwelling too much on this I turned it around to just think of Bruce flying all over the globe. I shared this thought on social media and my wonderful close friend Liz remarked *You handle your grief well*.

I like to think that I do but in private I can and do still fall apart and wish that Bruce could be with me.

In my Appendices (I to III) I include Bruce's last letter to me, Jane Patmore's tribute to him and my tribute to him.

As I believe sharing helps healing, in Appendix IV I include stories from people who have experienced loss and grief.

I do not discuss grief counselling in detail as this book is about my experience and how I cope. For some of you counselling will be beneficial and even necessary and should be sought if you are not coping with your loss. Help is available from medical, counselling, psychological and psychiatric professionals.

However, I also know that there can be long waiting lists for such help and even if you manage to find help it might be programs which are short term. So, I believe that you also need to have coping techniques that you can use to help you each day. This is where I hope that by sharing my experience and how I cope (as best I can) can help you if you use my coping tips and exercises (Appendix V). Other people offered to share with me their experiences of losing a loved one and I hope that sharing their stories (Appendix IV) will help too. Indeed, many have told me that sharing their story was a very therapeutic experience for them.

I am happy to receive constructive comments and contact which can be done through my website[14].

Sharing helps healing

I know from experience that having coping strategies to hand in the form of a book or other resource can help when coping with grief. So I developed MindBites[15] meditation videos and audios that can help relax, calm and help deal with challenges.

In Appendix V I share some information on controlling relationships and a brief overview of sociopathic and narcissistic behaviour. I also describe coping techniques which I developed. They are proven psychological techniques which, when used regularly, are very effective.

Finally, in Appendix VI, I provide some excerpts of blogs that were written before and after Bruce's death.

---

[14]   MindCircles www.mindcircles.co.uk
[15]   MindBites videos and audios www.stepsforsuccess.co.uk and www.mindcircles.co.uk

CHAPTER ONE

BRUCE – MY GORGEOUS BOY

*If given your time over again would you do things differently? I don't really know.
Hindsight is a great thing.*

The lives of our children are intertwined with those of their parents: the behaviour and actions of each impact on the other.

I want to share my experience of his birth as it was a long labour and when I lost him to suicide I started looking back over his whole life wondering if something had happened even in birth to cause problems in his later life. I am sure if you have lost a child you might do the same. I think I was seeking answers which even if they were found would not bring him back. In fact, answers could raise more questions and you could drive yourself mad.

As I said above it was a long labour but at the time all pain disappeared when this little bundle was placed in my arms. I know all mothers think their child is the most beautiful in the world and to me he was. I particularly loved his complexion which looked like he had holidayed in the sun. He looked so healthy compared to the other babies in the hospital! I did not realise at the time that the tan was due to new-born jaundice, which was caused by him having a high level of bilirubin which is a yellow pigment produced during the normal breakdown of red blood cells. The liver in new-borns is still developing and may not be mature enough to remove bilirubin. It often goes away on its own as the baby's liver develops and the baby starts to feed which helps the bilirubin pass through the body. It can be a serious condition but not in Bruce's case. To help him deal with the excess bilirubin, he was taken to the neo-natal unit in the hospital where he received phototherapy treatment. He was placed on a special bed under a blue spectrum light while wearing only a nappy and special protective goggles on his eyes.

Due to him being taken to the neo-natal unit, my adoptive parents arrived and my adoptive mother took my hand to comfort me, believing that something serious had happened to my baby boy. But what she said was so distressing: *'If it's God's will it's God's will'.* I could not believe what I was hearing. I was so upset and had to ask a nurse to take my mother out of the ward. It was only after her death that I understood the pain that my mother suffered of not giving birth to her own baby.

I only mention this as a reminder that none of us know what others are going through and I certainly did not know of my mother's anguish at that time (no excuse perhaps at the time but something I did eventually forgive her for). Looking now at the different 'faces' of Bruce I can see that I did not fully realise what he was going through at any one time. However, he was an actor and could—like many actors, particularly comedic actors—hide his feelings well.

Three faces of Bruce (sad, sombre, happy)

I know the circumstances around loss of a child are different depending on how the child died. In the case of suicide and I hope that by sharing what I feel, what I think about (searching for reasons even as far back as his birth) and what Bruce was like will go some way in helping bring comfort to you. Many of you may or hopefully will resonate with Bruce, my story and others who have shared their story on loss.

The reason for suicide is often never known and I will share later that a letter (Appendix I) from Bruce gave insight into his mind and reason.

However, if you are like me, I know that you will look back and wonder if there was something you could have done or changed that would have stopped your child from taking their own life.

I know I looked back (and still do, particularly in moments when the grief is just too heavy to bear), not just at the months before his death, but even reflecting on everything, from Bruce's birth to the day he died.

I drove myself mad by thinking and over thinking every situation, tiny or huge. I asked myself whether there was something that I could have done to change his mind but no matter how much I reflected it would not bring him back. So when I find myself reflecting I bring myself back into the present and hope with all my heart that he is at peace, a peace that he could not find in life.

It is important to understand that what parents do or do not do, impacts on all their children. It can impact to a greater extent on one child than another or so it might seem as all children will have their own story to tell and perhaps Bruce's siblings will one day share their stories. For now, it is about Bruce and my connection with him as his mother.

Have you ever chatted to your brothers, sisters, parents or family about a situation and there are shouts of *were you in the same family?* This is because we all see situations from our own perspective which might be very different from others in the family.

My knowledge of his life and how he felt about his life comes from my personal experience as his mother and from both my own and his diaries. I was also informed by my many conversations with him over the years, particularly those years leading up to his tragic decision to commit suicide.

As his mother I am obviously biased but considering all those who contacted me after his death and who attended the celebration of his life I know they felt the same about him as me. I don't think he realised just how many people loved him.

It is impossible to detail every aspect of Bruce's life in this book but I will share as much as I can about his life and how situations—which on hindsight might have been avoided— impacted on this sensitive soul.

Bruce's early years

Have you ever looked at your child and thought they have been here before? He was a quiet baby. He had a quiet, soulful, knowing look about him. I often felt that he had *been here before*. Even as a baby he was creative and quite happy to sit alone playing with toys, boxes, whatever was to hand. He would get really upset if people shouted and this continued into adulthood; he never liked confrontation.

They say a picture says a thousand words, so I ask you to look back at the collage at the start of the book. I put this together for the celebration of his life. Now I know you will probably need a magnifying glass to view the pictures, but it is worthwhile as you will see the many faces of Bruce.

He started to speak when he was very young (but I hear you say every parent says this about their child!) Some of his words could be clearly recognised but he also had a language he shared with his younger brother who was born only 11 months later.

He loved drawing and painting, even trying to write his own stories. Although he was happy to play on his own, he enjoyed being at playgroup. His creative ideas filled his head so much that often throughout his life he would say *Mummy I feel as if my head is going to explode*. I can empathise with this.

From some of our conversations when he came back to stay in Glasgow I realised that he did not fully understand just how much he meant to me as my first born child. Having left home and not been in daily contact he thought that his role of being the oldest in the family had been taken over by his younger brother. It did not help that he looked younger than his siblings! Oh, how many would wish to look younger but for Bruce in many ways he wanted to look the part as the older brother. No matter how many times I told him that he would always be my first born he found it difficult to accept.

When he was born I just wanted to hold him and cuddle him. Many years later he told me he would have loved to have been an only child. When I look back I knew what he meant, recalling that I had treated him as much older than his 'baby' years particularly when his brother came along only 11 months later, followed by a sister 11 months later and then another sister.

I get upset and angry with myself and feel guilty when I remember telling him, at the age of only 2 or 3 years old, that he was the oldest and didn't need to be carried like a baby! But he *was* just a baby! Anyone who has lots of children will no doubt resonate with this. However, when one loses a child you think back on all those times and wish you could take back these words.

> *But hindsight is a wonderful thing!*

I had always wanted lots of children. Before the youngest of my four children was born I had three children under the age of three, so life was always hectic. We lived in a village and my neighbours were very supportive. However, family life even then was not always idyllic and when I look back the children always had to be in bed before their father came home.

When I look back, I think that my decision to marry was because I was seeking a way out of my own situation at that time. But of course if I had not married I would not have ended up with four wonderful children.

I remember, shortly after my marriage, telling my adoptive father that I had made a mistake, but he just said, *'You made your bed you lie in it'.* I made a decision then to make the best of my marriage and have children on whom I could lavish all my love and up until the point where my husband and I separated, that is what I did my best to do.

When Bruce was an adult I used to have discussions about his father. We never really reached a conclusion other than in my opinion his father wanted to control everything and everyone around him. Bruce was an avid reader of psychology books and academic articles and tried to find out if his father had certain personality traits.

If you feel or find yourself in a controlling and toxic relationship and can empathise with my experience I recommend that you seek professional advice to help you take care of yourself and not fall into the trap of similar relationships in the future. As for me, I wish I had sought professional advice or *'walked away'* earlier but this proved easier said than done.

Having had a difficult, some would say 'strange' upbringing where my elderly adoptive parents showed love by spending money on me, I knew that I did not want this kind of love for my children. However, the upside of being brought up in this way was that I had a good education which included learning piano, violin, ballet, elocution and drama which was to stand me in good stead for the future.

Another factor that was to my advantage was my 'bloody-minded gene'! My adoptive father often told me that I had this gene! If I was told I could not do something then I would prove that I could. So, when he told me to make my bed and lie in it, my bloody-minded gene kicked in and I told myself that I would make the best of a bad situation (my marriage). I had always wanted children, so I knew then what to do. I was going to have my own children that I would love and I did—four wonderful children, two boys and two girls which I would not change for the world.

Bruce's other main talent besides photography was swimming. Like me, he was not keen on team sports, preferring to excel on his own and in his own way, and he did, winning the 'Under 16s' Championship and many other swimming galas. He practiced at every opportunity.

Some of Bruce's swimming medals

Because I had three other children, I decided that we could all take part if I became part of a swimming coaching team. This meant that all four children became adept at swimming and won medals too.

However, when I reflect on Bruce's talent for swimming I wonder if I could have done more to promote this talent: could he have been an Olympic swimmer?

I am sure others who lose a child will empathise with this. When you suffer the tragic loss of a loved one, particularly, a child there is, or seems to be, as in my case, a need to look back and wonder.

Could I have done more?
Would Bruce's life have taken a different route?
Could I have avoided his tragic decision?

Difficult decisions

During the early years of Bruce and his siblings I had difficult decisions to make. Try as I could my marriage was not in a good way, to put it mildly. I struggled on trying to avoid confrontation and keep things as calm as possible for the children, especially Bruce who was greatly affected.

We moved from the small village to the outskirts of the city and to a bigger house. I had hoped that this move and the birth of my youngest child, a baby girl, would make a difference. Sadly it made no difference to my marriage but as always I was at my happiest when there was just me and the children and we had wonderful times together.

Years later my close friend told me she believed that the move, in her opinion, had been a deliberate one made by my husband to isolate me from friends. Whether that was the case or not, my married life continued to be less than idyllic. However, at this point I was still determined to make a go of things. I even tried to speak with my husband about the marriage on many occasions, but it always seemed to fall on deaf ears. For a long time, I swayed from wondering whether I should stay for the sake of the children or leave for their sake (and mine). I knew that it was going to be a difficult decision.

However, this decision was made for me when Bruce saw a confrontation between his father and me. I heard Bruce's small voice say, *'Mummy we have to leave'*. It was hearing the anxiety in his voice and the fear in his eyes I decided that we had to leave.

I had hoped that sensibility would prevail and that my husband and I could agree on a divorce and access to all four children. Sadly, this was not to be, and it took 10 years before matters were settled. This took its toll on me (not that I realised it at the time because I thought I was *'super-human (woman)'* and I found it difficult during these years to cope with everything, looking after the needs of myself and my children.

During the divorce years, access to the four children was sporadic and when I look back, I think that these years had probably affected Bruce more than his younger brother and sisters but I did not realise it at the time.

Fortunately I was living with the children at that time in a townhouse type property and the neighbours were all supportive and sympathetic to my situation and where possible they babysat or child minded if I had made arrangements to go out which was not often as I tended to invite my friends over to my flat rather than go out. On other occasions I was left with no alternative but to take the children with me. So, it was a free-spirited, bohemian kind of lifestyle which I believe we enjoyed together. Indeed, Bruce's brother and sisters referred to this lifestyle when talking with the celebrant about what she would say in her tribute to Bruce (Appendix II).

During those difficult years I did not realise, at the time, how exhausting it had been and that it would later take its toll on me and the children. To this day I do not think that my ex-husband has any idea what these years did to me or the children. On reading Bruce's last letter (Appendix I) to me in my opinion the lengthy divorce process had affected him more than I or anyone realised.

If I was to be asked if I had any regrets, then I would probably say that if I had my time over again I would have focused more on my children instead of trying to keep income coming in by working hard or for too many hours. But as I have said before, hindsight is a great thing.

My main reason for deciding to leave was that I did not want my children to grow up in an argumentative, confrontational, emotionally (and physically) abusive environment.

I know that many of you will understand and even resonate with my situation but despite this, and in light of what happened to Bruce, I often wonder if I should have tried to stay in the family home for the children's sake. I keep going over questions such as:

Would life have been better for them all instead of uprooting them?

Would things have turned out differently for Bruce?

Who knows? I didn't stay. I left, believing that it was for the best. Worse was to come. I did not know at the time of leaving that the divorce would be acrimonious and take 10 years to resolve. Sadly, by that time, even with a settlement, I was left with huge debts.

I felt it necessary to talk about life as it was for me and why I made my decision. However, this is more about how Bruce saw life before and after we left.

When Bruce returned to Glasgow we did manage to talk about how he felt before we left the family home. He said that all he could remember when we lived as a family was not being understood by his father.

Some things he talked about I was not aware of. He told me about incidents of walking home from swimming practice with no money and seeing his father fly past in his big, fancy car! At the time he kept such incidents to himself so I did not realise how hurt he was.

As I said earlier Bruce talked from an early age. He loved reading and his passion for reading continued into his adulthood. He would devour books on all kinds of topics, particularly history, politics but best of all anything to do with art.

As a child he would doodle and draw on anything! Later he would draw character figures for an idea he had of life with his brother and used the special language they shared when babies, calling them 'gaino' and 'gaddow' and remembering 'stoombie away home'

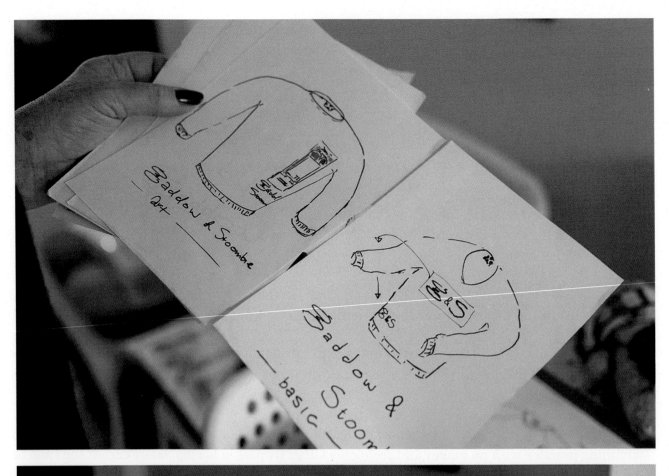

Bruce & his brother as cartoon characters: drawn by Bruce

Bruce always liked doing things on his own, particularly if it was a creative pursuit. He was not keen on being told to do something by an authority figure especially if that person had less knowledge and experience than Bruce. Research shows that a person who is averse to being controlled by an authority figure makes a good entrepreneur. In this respect Bruce did have entrepreneurial spirit but unlike his brother he did not possess the commercial, business head for making money which he might have successfully done from his art and photography.

If only he had been able to work with his more commercially minded brother then Bruce's work could have sold worldwide. But it was not to be.

If only…. How many times do we say that?

When I look back Bruce possessed the same bloody-minded gene as me.

If only he used this gene in a more constructive way rather than being stubborn, wanting to do everything his way.

I do empathise with creative people. As a creative person myself I know that when I create something, a painting, even this book, I am seeking perfection so much so that I keep re-doing and re-thinking. Bruce was the same, never satisfied with his own work. It did not matter if I, or anyone else, told him it was good, he would want to re-paint, re-sculpt, re-photograph!

I am fortunate that I am able to listen to trusted friends when they say enough is enough—just leave it as it is! I would quietly accept and instead of my bloody-minded gene holding me back I would let it kick in and tell myself that I will succeed.

Bruce was not able to do this. He would not accept words from others, even words of support—everything had to be perfect in his eyes. I know that being like this drove him 'mad' but still he could not change.

Bruce, like me, also had a rebellious streak. I knew Bruce would not be suited to a regular nine to five job and I was right. When working between acting gigs he loved working on construction sites which offered him not just money but flexibility to work on his passion; his acting, painting or photography.

I have lectured for many years and I always gravitated towards those who had a rebellious streak. I saw the potential in many and found that they showed more intelligence than they were given credit for. I found many to be creative with the ability to think out of the box.

Bruce's love of books and his avid reading on many topics would also be a source of hurt later in his life. He told me that on many occasions, if there was a discussion about a topic of which he had knowledge, he would eagerly share that knowledge believing that sharing his opinion would be welcomed. However, his views were often dismissed and he was regarded as either arrogant or a 'know it all'. He could not understand why people would not want to know more or have different views on a topic. He was anything but arrogant and was only being himself, sharing his knowledge. He could not understand how inputting his thoughts (usually true facts) on a topic would cause such anger in some people. I tried to tell him that some people might feel undermined by what they saw (incorrectly) as arrogance.

One such occasion comes to mind. When Bruce returned to Glasgow, he enrolled in a photography course at a nearby college and loved the fact that being a student gave him access to some amazing equipment. However, once again his problem with 'authority' figures raised its ugly head. I knew he was upset and when I asked him why he told me that he had annoyed a lecturer because he had shared with this person his knowledge that he had of the subject matter. He was told not to be disruptive and to be quiet. Bruce failed to understand this as he thought the lecturer could have shared a discussion with him on the topic. I told Bruce that sometimes some lecturers might not know something and are afraid to make students aware of their lack of knowledge. Often what is required now in some educational institutions is for students to listen and repeat what they have learned in class. Bruce was astounded by this. He said he thought tertiary education was about learning and extending knowledge not just regurgitating something a lecturer has said. I could understand both perspectives. As a lecturer some students are always trying to challenge your knowledge. Fortunately, I am confident enough to tell them that I don't know everything, but I do know where to find the answer. I also know that I liked students who were challenging and a debate could arise bringing out more information on a topic. Sadly, this is not something many lecturers are comfortable with. Bruce was fortunate in that while undertaking his studies he was able to overcome such challenges and met a wonderful man Martin Gilfeather who became his mentor and friend. Bruce graduated, which was a very proud moment for me.

Bruce's graduation

Bruce also had a cultured voice, due to his training in acting and was very talented in different accents. However, his cultured voice became another challenge to overcome as this accent was not well-received when he returned to his hometown. On more than one occasion he was told he was a snob. Again, he could not understand why having a different accent from others could be a problem and this caused him hurt. Funnily enough later when working on construction sites to earn more income to support his art and photography he was able to use his talent for different accents which made him accepted and well-liked by his fellow workers.

Anyone who is an actor or artist will know that it is difficult to make a living. Despite Bruce's many photographs, writings, artwork and his entrepreneurial spirit he did not have the business or commercial brain for making money from his work. There are many situations where he could have made money but could not bring himself to let go of his work.

Bruce's sculptures

Bruce's sculpture exhibition leaflet

Bruce created sculptures, using silver and velvet. I recall one occasion when he was persuaded to hold an exhibition showcasing his work. This first exhibition was a great success with people loving his work and many wanting or indeed buying the various pieces. However, instead of being delighted he got quite upset. When I asked him why he said that he found it difficult to let go of his sculptures; what he considered as his 'babies'. I understand this as I can feel that way about my work: I want my books to be bought but I still find it difficult to take criticism of my 'babies' as I am sure many of you will agree if someone criticises your children or someone you love.

Bruce liked to work alone and was fiercely independent and protective about his art, no matter the medium he was working in, be that sculpting, painting, writing, acting or eventually his photography. He needed and wanted space—indeed what most artists want—space to create. However, those who successfully sell their work are able to let go of their work, sell it or find an agent to take on the business side of promoting the work. This was not the case for Bruce; as far as his creative work was concerned he found it difficult (even impossible) to work with anyone else—not even his brother who has a head for business—to promote or sell his work.

However, as far as creative projects other than his art or photography Bruce was very happy to work with his brother, whether that was building or demolition work. They were fondly known as Botchit and Scarper. In fact, as I mentioned above when they were babies, they had their own language, often talking to each other in phrases such as *'gainos, gadoes, stoombie away home'*!

Teenage years - the turning point for Bruce

I often wish that I had spent more time with my children rather than trying to work to support them. It saddens me to think back about how I had also been conditioned as a child to believe that *'a woman needs a man'*. This conditioning is not an excuse but goes some way to understand why I made poor relationship choices. I wrote about the effects of past-conditioning in my *7 Attributes for Success (Inner Success and Happiness)*[16] book and more recently in my *Resilience and Courage: the Key to Endurance*[17] book and the importance of understanding the impact (usually or often negative). The stories about my life are for another book but suffice to say that one relationship led to a rift between Bruce and me. Worse than that was his decision to leave and go to live with his father, shouting at me that *'he would be loved'*.

Looking back, I believe this was the turning point in Bruce's life. I hoped that perhaps living with his father, as an 'only' child would be best and that he would be loved. I was to find out later that this was not the case and that life with his father was not idyllic.

Years later Bruce told me that his father had said to him in no uncertain terms: *'Remember this is my house and not your home!'*

This raises another huge regret of mine: that I did not go to his father's house and bring Bruce home. But as I said before, Bruce and I are very alike. We are both stubborn and do not back down when a decision is made. However, Bruce was right when he told me many years later *'Mum, you were the adult'*. He was right—I should have been the adult and brought him back home to me and his siblings.

Hindsight is a great thing!

A few years passed, and managing to put poor relationships behind me, I met someone and it was at that time Bruce's brother arranged for Bruce to come to lunch with everyone. There were more tears at that lunch than ever before but they were tears of happiness for me as Bruce was back in my life, albeit not back staying in Glasgow but at least he was making his own way (or so I thought) in London. I would go down to London to meet him but I saw that his life was not a bed of roses. Bruce told me that in order to access money from his bank account he needed permission from his father. Now it may be that his father did this with the best of intentions but Bruce felt that he was still being controlled by his father leaving him no choice but to ask for money when or if he needed it.

---

[16]   Elliot, Patricia (2010) *7 Attributes for Success (Inner Success and Happiness)* Authorhouse, available on www.mindcircles.co.uk and Amazon

[17]   Elliot, Patricia (2020) *Resilience and Courage: the Key to Endurance* Authorhouse, available on www.mindcircles.co.uk

I know from my conversations with Bruce that he was not an 'angel' and that he did smoke 'weed' but more than that he also drank too much, and I believe the combination of these impacted on him. He worked as a waiter and sometimes as a chef in some of the best bars and restaurants in London and he became very aware of the importance of healthy eating which continued to the end of his life.

All four of my children are very different which is not unusual. However, I noticed that as Bruce became a teenager he started to assert himself which was a good thing, but he also became a very angry young man. Sometimes his anger became physical and on one notable occasion we did come to blows. I told him this needed to stop and that his behaviour was unacceptable. This row was what led him to telling me that he was going to go to his father's home where he believed he would be loved. Part of me hoped that he would be loved but in my heart I knew that this might not be so. I was in shock when he left and wanted to rush out and bring him home, but I also thought he would walk off his anger and return home to me. He did not.

I discovered that he had indeed gone to his father's house. I consoled myself with the thought that he would be loved and treated like an 'only' child with more attention than I could give him when I had four of them with me.

It was only when we were re-united that I learned he did not get the love he so desperately wanted from his father. This ripped my heart apart and once again I wished I had brought him home.

If only.........

Until the day he died, Bruce would often tell me that he could not understand why his father did not understand how his actions had affected him. All Bruce sought over the years was an apology from his father. He was even angry that his brother and sisters did not see how their father behaved towards all of them.

I often told Bruce that the best form of revenge is to be happy and succeed in whatever you do but that success had nothing to do with having lots of money. It was about inner happiness and success. I know Bruce took my words on board as he helped me when I was writing my *7 Attributes for Success book*[18] by often giving me tips on how to feel good. However, despite giving me these tips he was not able to apply them himself and could not overcome the intense anger against his father. This anger often invaded his thoughts. These led him to despair and bouts of low moods. All he wanted was his father to apologise. I told Bruce that I did not believe that an apology would ever be made and that he had to come to terms with this. Sadly, over the years Bruce could not accept this and ultimately, I believe this led to his decision to end his life. My belief is confirmed by his words in his final letter (Appendix I) to me.

Bruce's anger was not just directed at his father, but also at me. Fortunately for me, when we reconciled we were able to talk about how angry he had been at me, asking me why I had not come for him when he went to his father's house. I told him I sincerely believed and really thought that he would be loved as an 'only' child but was horrified when he told me how he had been treated. I told him I was truly sorry that I had not brought him home and that I would regret that decision until the day I died.

---

[18]   Elliot, Patricia (2010) *7 Attributes for Success (Inner Success and Happiness)* Authorhouse available on www.mindcircles.co.uk and Amazon

Unfortunately, like his father Bruce seemed to have a tendency to blame things from his past and I used to tell him that he could not change the past, but he can change how he views the past.

In my opinion, if only Bruce's father had accepted blame (or some blame), apologised and been able to have conversations with Bruce about the anger he felt against him, I believe things could have turned out differently.

If only........hindsight is a great thing

Years lost?

I knew there would be so much to catch up on, but I was not prepared for how much Bruce had suffered since being separated from me and his siblings.

I had always known that Bruce was creative like me, but I did not realise the extent of Bruce's creativity until I went through his belongings after his death. These included books, writings, artwork, poems, notes from his studies and his travels.

I knew that Bruce had lived and worked in London for some years. He had a loving relationship with a Danish girl and despite them eventually deciding to part company, they remained friends throughout. I know she was heart-broken by his death.

I don't think Bruce was ready to settle down but there was more to it than that. He would tell me that he was worried about having children in case they inherited his 'difficult' gene! He also said that if he did have children it would be one child, upon whom he would pour all his love. However, this was not to be, and he is now gone leaving no 'little' one in whom I could see Bruce's traits and character.

CHAPTER TWO

REUNITED – OPENING PANDORA'S BOX

I remember the moment like it was yesterday. A phone call from a call box— it was Bruce. I could hear from his voice that he was not in a good way but before he could tell me what was wrong the phone went dead. I realised that something was wrong as I had received a poem from him and when I read it out to some young people that I was working with and who had struggled with drugs and homelessness, one young girl was very moved and said, *'that person is in a bad way, they are struggling and probably homeless'.* I had not told them that the poem had been written by my son.

This hit me hard and although worried I could do little about it as I had no phone or address details for Bruce. While living in London he had moved two or three times. I visited one of his flats but I knew he had moved from there.

I prayed that Bruce would phone me back and my prayers were answered. This time I heard his voice, it was like the little boy all those years ago: *'Mummy can I come home?'* Of course I did not hesitate and told him I would love to have him home. I arranged for him, his books and belongings to come home to me. My decision caused some tension with his siblings as they knew I only had a small flat and in their opinion as an adult Bruce should have been capable of sorting out his own life. Nonetheless, I told them that no matter their age, if any of my children was in trouble then I was their mother and I would happily have them home.

I couldn't wait for the door to open and see my boy again, my baby who was now some six feet tall. Bruce had always been thin but I was not prepared for how gaunt he looked. I also did not know that opening the door to Bruce was to be like opening Pandora's box or should I say I wish it had opened Pandora's box immediately but it was to be many months before I realised how he had been living and even then, some parts of his life were not discovered until after his death.

Again, I am left with the feeling, *'If only ....'*

All I could think of at the time was 'My Bruce had come home to me'. Little did I realise that it was not the Bruce that I knew as a baby. Yes, he still had his lovely smile, his creative thoughts but life had damaged him; damage that I hoped could be mended by him coming home to me.

Over the months we were able to openly talk about things that had happened in the past. He shared his love of acting and some of his acting roles. I eagerly asked him what roles he was considering for the future but it was then he told me about his 'stage fright' experience which led him to leave acting. He had frozen on stage when being the lead in a play in London and he just could not get over it. He decided then that his life would be behind the camera and not in front of it.

Bruce had always wanted to pursue an acting career. He told me when he lived in London he was successful in gaining acting roles. However, as any actor knows these roles alone do not provide enough income to make a living, so to increase his income Bruce worked in bars, restaurants and hotels. Indeed, his brother told me that when he visited Bruce in London he was working at one of the top hotels and could have made a career in that field. However, Bruce being Bruce wanted to pursue a career in acting. Here are some excerpts from his acting along with some casting photos of his time in London and LA.

Bruce – various acting roles

The downside to working in bars was that Bruce enjoyed a drink. He shared with me that he wished he could be like those people who are satisfied after one or two drinks but, sadly, Bruce was someone who did not know when to stop. We often discussed this and whether it might be because he had an addictive gene. Addiction has been the topic of much research, but I think the jury is still out on whether an addictive gene exists. What is known is that addicts can become addicted to many things from alcohol and drugs to shopping and more.

Bruce's drinking seriously worried me particularly since it made him a very angry person. I also learned that he smoked cannabis (weed) and that made him calm. However, watching the effects of the combination of drink and weed I was left in no doubt that the drinking had far greater effects on him than smoking weed. When he was drunk, he would become angry, talk too loudly and ended up alienating others.

When he returned home he lived with me for a while and during that time I saw how pained and distraught he was. He would say to me that his head felt so full sometimes that it was as if it would explode. It was as if he was 'high' not on drugs but on creativity. I knew how he felt as sometimes my head seems so full of creative ideas but somehow I am able to compartmentalise my ideas and thoughts; something which Bruce just did not seem able to do or even want to do. He used to say that it was only when he felt 'high' that he could function more creatively. I saw and felt his pain and as a Mum just wanted to hug him and take his pain away.

On some occasions he would tell me that he felt his brain operated differently from others. At these times he would ask me why I had not had him diagnosed with bi-polar disorder. Again I would reflect and wonder if I should have done something about his anger in his teenage years but I just thought it was teenage behaviour and that he would outgrow it. I did not know that he had many highs and lows throughout his life and it was only after his death when I read through some of his many notebooks that I learned of just how distraught he was at times.

As time passes by, I do but write to satisfy my mind! Bruce Macleod

Whether I could have stopped him from drinking too much or smoking weed is something I will never know and of course even if I had wanted him to stop, only he as an individual could do so and he did seek help. He would stop drinking for weeks at a time but start again. However, in the two years prior to his death he told me that he had been sober and I knew this to be so as I did see a difference in him.

Going through his notebooks and papers after his death I found out that he had sought help for what he believed was a mental health issue. He visited various medical professionals but this merely resulted in him being given prescription drugs. He took these drugs for a few weeks but he found them to dull his brain and, in his view, take away his creativity.

When he returned home to me he signed up as a patient to a local medical practice. He told me he really liked the doctor and that they had some really good conversations. However, I realised Bruce enjoyed talking with the doctor as their conversations were more about mental health issues than finding out how to help Bruce other than with prescription drugs. So once again Bruce would try taking the drugs for a few weeks, but the effect was as before; his brain was dulled and he seemed to lose his creativity I noticed the change as he looked like a 'zombie' and was certainly not the highly spirited, creative boy I knew. I could understand why he did not want to take such drugs and of course he stopped and he was proved correct: his creativity returned, but at the cost of mood swings.

There were many things I discovered when he returned home. From London he moved to Los Angeles where he joined an acting academy, resulting in roles in various films, some of which won awards at Cannes film festival. Contrary to what many people may think, such awards do not mean that those involved are making lots of money. The fees for the Academy were too much for Bruce, despite working in bars and restaurants over there. I know from his notes that he asked his father for money to complete the course but this money was not forthcoming. I do wish he had asked me, but he knew at that time that I would not have had the money to support him and being a thoughtful soul, he had decided not to ask me.

Despite Bruce seeming reserved he made friends wherever he went and this was highlighted by the number of friends attending his celebration of life and those across the globe who could not attend but contacted me after his death. I don't think Bruce realised how much he was loved by so many people.

After his time in LA Bruce returned to London and continued his career as an actor, gaining roles, one of which was as King Lear in a West End play.

He still had to supplement his income by working in bars and restaurants, the upside of which brought him close friends who had no idea of the inner struggles that Bruce had and this was evident by their shock on hearing of his suicide. His long-term girlfriend and close friends told me they reflected on their time with Bruce and ask themselves if they should have been aware of his struggles and whether there was more they could have done. I think it is normal for people in close relationships to reflect when they lose someone, particularly to suicide.

After his death I found in his many notebooks the lines that he needed to learn for his acting roles. This was his way of learning his lines. Interestingly enough it was how I used to learn and one of his nieces does this too.

From actor to photographer

Why the change? As any actor knows it is not easy to make a living from being an actor and many need to supplement their income. I did know this but had no idea how lack of income impacted on Bruce as much as it had. Bruce also shared with me that it was not just the lack of income but that he had suffered stage fright during one of his roles on stage in the West End. This combination resulted in Bruce making the choice to instead be behind the camera instead of in front of it.

Returning home to me was not easy for Bruce and in addition to this he had no acting roles or jobs lined up, so he had to 'sign on' to receive government benefit payment. This process required completing multiple forms to demonstrate that he was actively looking for jobs. This caused Bruce a lot of distress as he found filling in forms difficult due to what I think (in hindsight) was dyslexia. On one occasion he called me to say that he had been ejected from the job centre as he had been angry at how he had been treated. It seemed that he started to fill out a form with his name and address when the assistant whipped the form out of his hands saying that this part of the form was to be completed by staff. The assistant returned with another form and started to insert Bruce's name and address where he had done so in the previous form. Bruce got so frustrated and angry that the security guard was called and told to remove him from the building. Fortunately, the security guard was very understanding and calmed Bruce down. Such situations got Bruce angry because to him they were petty.

Living with me in a small flat was also hard for Bruce. He said he felt ashamed that he had to come home. He felt a failure as he was not as successful as his siblings. No matter how much I told him this was untrue and that I was happy to have him home, those feelings persisted in him.

Knowing how keen he was to pursue a career in photography we discussed the possibility of him studying in this field. He decided to enrol on a photography course and indeed graduated—a very proud Mum moment.

Following graduation, Bruce got his own flat near the Art School in Glasgow. It was on the top floor with access to the roof where you could sit and view the whole city. It was light and bright; ideal for Bruce to create his photography. The downside was that it was rather small for some of Bruce's ideas! His dream was to have a loft area extending over many metres. However, he created some amazing photography including fashion which can be seen from the images reproduced here.

Bruce's fashion photography

Despite his photography he found it increasingly difficult to bring in enough income. Bruce also learned that when studying at college or university, students have access to amazing and expensive professional equipment for photographic shoots but when students leave their studies, this equipment is not readily available so they have to either purchase or hire their own equipment. In addition to doing this Bruce had to have insurance to cover the equipment as well as professional indemnity insurance. All these come at a cost, most of which is too much for a budding entrepreneur so they often have no alternative but to rely on family to cover the cost or obtain another job to support their photography.

This is where Bruce's lack of business acumen showed through. He was still not willing (or able) to let someone else guide him towards the possibility of selling his photography. He managed to obtain freelance work for a well-known newspaper, photographing Andrew Miller[19] and Lucy Reeves[20]. This both excited him and led to some more work. He had hoped that it would lead to full-time position but sadly this was not to be.

In order to pursue his photography Bruce needed extra jobs to bring in income but these jobs would also need to be flexible to allow for his creative pursuits. Such jobs tended to be in the construction sites; none of which were full-time or permanent positions. These temporary jobs were ideal for Bruce and he obtained the necessary certificates to allow him to work on construction sites. His varied experiences on such sites and meeting with all different types of people added to Bruce's creative ideas for photography. He loved the different angles and shapes of buildings and took many photographs on the sites and of buildings in the many places he worked and visited across the UK and abroad. Here are some of his photographs.

---

[19]   Miller, Andrew *One Morning Like a Bird, interview The Herald, 6 September 2008 (photograph by Bruce Macleod)*
[20]   Reeves, Lucy *Muddy Matches, interview The Herald Magazine, 14 February 2009 (photograph by Bruce Macleod)*

Bruce's photography various photos of Scotland, Cuba and New York

Bruce's brain was never quiet and he was forever working out different ways of using his photography. He was visually aware of his surroundings, always finding obscure information on walls of buildings whether in Glasgow or further afield in his travels. His visits to Cuba produced amazing photographs of the everyday life of people as well as the architecture. As well as Cuba, Bruce photographed unusual aspects of many places on his travels, such as New York and LA.

In addition to his love of buildings and their structure, he loved the more unusual types of fashion photography, such as the works of Iris Brosch[21]. He admired and was influenced by her work so imagine his excitement when he was asked to assist her in some shoots.

Psychoactive photographer

After his death, a close friend helped me access his computer which opened up even more aspects of Bruce through the many, varied photographs. Just before his death Bruce had compiled certain photographs and text into a book he called *Psychoactive Photographer*. He was in discussion with a bookstore about publishing his book. He was so excited and I believed that his life was turning for the better and that he would get recognition for his photography. Sadly this was not to be. I show some of these below and hope that one day I will manage to publish that book[22].

21   Brosch, Iris https://vimeo.com/irisbrosch
22   Macleod, Bruce *Psychoactive Photographer (tbc)*

Bruce's psychoactive photos from his book (floating book, Beethoven, The dark dolls)

I have no doubts that Bruce knew himself well and had carefully chosen the title of his book. During the years he lived back with me and then when he lived in his own flat beside the Art School I could not ignore his problems and how troubled he was. These all pointed to mental health problems. Being passionate about activities of the mind and helping people realise their true potential I was eager to help my son. However, this is easier said than done. It is difficult for some people to talk about their mental health and this was especially so for Bruce. However, Bruce could talk about the topic of mental health, even helping me develop techniques for the mind for my book *7 Attributes for Success* and my business MindCircles. As I recall our chats about his visits with the doctor I realised that he was not talking about his own mental health issues but more generally trying to find ways of helping others deal with such issues.

After his death I found his copious notes, and they showed that he had tried to find answers. One such search was his writing on a poem by Ella Wheeler Wilcox[23]: *Answered Prayers* – an excerpt from the poem:

> *.......I prayed for a contented mind. At length great light upon my darkened spirit burst Great peace fell on me also, and great strength – oh, had that prayer been first.*

In our discussions I realised that Bruce was well read on mental health. He had also consulted medical professionals, doctors and psychiatrists as well as going on yoga retreats all to help him with his mind. As I said above, from my discussions with him about his visits with medical professionals I realised that he was talking with them on an 'academic' level rather than trying to find ways of helping him. He was prescribed drugs for what the doctors believed was depression but these left him feeling like a zombie. It was heart-rending when I saw him like this. He openly said that these drugs took away his creativity and left him feeling 'bland'.

Following a visit to one yoga retreat he said that he found the experience uplifting at first but as the days went by he found it increasingly difficult to 'clear his mind' which was the purpose of the retreat. Many who do yoga and use mindfulness techniques will know that clearing the mind can be very difficult.

On listening to Bruce talk about his difficulty in clearing his mind I could resonate with him. Being a creative person, my head is sometimes so full of ideas that I feel as if it could explode and I too can find it very difficult to clear my mind. It takes a lot of effort to do so and knowing Bruce I just knew he would find this too hard. So when he returned home, the uplifting feeling quickly dissipated and he was left feeling even more anxious. This resulted once more in him turning to alcohol and smoking cannabis.

I wanted to get him help but when your child is an adult (at 16 years old in Scotland) then you can only offer to help if the person actively seeks their own help. This is quite disturbing. What is even more worrying is that on one occasion when Bruce had got so worked up that he smashed his head against the door and then rushed out. I was worried about what he might do to himself, so I phoned his brother who told me he knew where to find him. Some hours later Bruce's brother phoned to tell me that all was well—he had found Bruce—but when trying to calm him down, a passing taxi driver thought they were two drunks fighting and shouted that he was going to get the police. Bruce's brother told him to

---

[23]   Wilcox, Ella Wheeler *Answered Prayers* The Freeport Press (OH) 8 Nov 1883:7

do so. The police duly arrived but attempted to arrest both of them. Fortunately Bruce's brother was able to explain what was happening and they said that they would take Bruce back to the police station where he would be seen by a psychologist. When I heard about this, my heart lifted and I thought at last Bruce would get help.

How wrong could I be. Believing that he would see a psychologist but not certain that this would be so, I phoned my doctor friend who told me that this was not the case as there were no psychologists at the police station. I was very worried and decided to phone the local police stations only to find out that Bruce was not there. One station said Bruce had been taken to the hospital. I then phoned round the local hospitals only to find out that Bruce had been seen in accident and emergency by a doctor but released as they found nothing wrong with him.

According to his brother, Bruce had been warned by the police to stay away from my house. However, a few hours passed and Bruce arrived home, pleased as punch telling me that he was not mental as he was intelligent enough to manipulate the situation at the police station whereby he was released from the police and taken to the hospital. He was then clever enough to manipulate the doctor so he was released by the doctor too. In short, this was the problem. Bruce was an educated individual and could use his intelligence when needed to manipulate more or less any situation. I have no doubts that his educated, intelligent conversations with his medical professionals would leave them with the belief that Bruce was mentally stable. For my part I think his mental health problems arose from his drinking, even more so than smoking any cannabis. His drinking caused upset because it made his mood swing to extreme anger. As I said before, he often repeated that he wished he could drink like others, where he could just have a couple of drinks and be happy at that.

Bruce realised on a few occasions that his drinking had to stop, and he joined the local Alcoholics Anonymous (AA) with a view to it helping him. This did not last long as he felt that he could 'do it alone'.

There were times when Bruce would stop drinking for months which shows that he had will power when he wanted. He managed to be alcohol free for about two years prior to his death and when I spoke with the pathologist, I was told that Bruce was free from alcohol and drugs. This of course left me with the question—why the decision to end his life?

The answer (or at least part) was to come from his letter (Appendix I) to me.

I have thought long and hard about writing about Bruce's faults. I find it painful to reflect on these. I know I, like others, have faults but when my beloved son is gone it is even more difficult to not only face the fact that he had faults but also talk about them. Like any Mum, I don't want to think of my children as having any faults. So, you can imagine that when it comes to talking about faults in Bruce I find tears leaking out of my eyes and rolling down my cheeks.

Later on in this book I talk about problems and troubles that should not be ignored and give some tips to help in situations where you are anxious and frightened that your child might be contemplating suicide.

I also include stories (Appendix IV) that others have shared with me about the loss of a loved one and I am honoured and privileged to have received them to include them in this book.

CHAPTER THREE

IF ONLY...WHAT IF?... GUT FEELINGS?... TURNING POINTS?

Hindsight is a great thing
Never ignore your gut feeling if you feel something is not right, it probably is not right.

What has gut feeling got to do with my son's suicide? Well it has and I should have gone with my gut feelings throughout his life.

When someone commits suicide questions that people often ask include some of the following.

Did you know?

Did you have any idea that they might do this?

Were there any signs?

Have they tried it before?

When people ask such questions it triggers thoughts that somehow you should have or must have known something was wrong. You rack your brains to try to remember if there were signs. More than this you start thinking that there were signs even as far back as birth. You berate yourself for ignoring them and not acting on these signs.

You look back at the whole life of your child.

Did I miss something even at birth?

My labour with Bruce was very long and immediately at birth he was taken to the pre-natal unit. This was due to his colour (which I thought was very healthy looking – as if he had been on holiday!) but the colour meant he had 'new-born jaundice'. This is when a new-born has a high level of bilirubin, a yellow pigment produced during the breakdown of red blood cells. His liver was not mature enough to remove bilirubin. It is of course quite common and would (should) not affect his later life but I still find myself wondering if it had any influence on him.

I looked back at all the times he had fallen.

Did he bump his head so hard that this did something to his brain?

So many questions and no real answers.

I wanted to honestly say that over the years I had no idea that Bruce had or might have had suicidal thoughts. However, after my tragic loss I wanted to make sense of it all. I wanted to look back to see if there were signs but I really didn't want to look back just in case there was something I could have done to prevent his suicide.

Then, painful though it was and whether I wanted to or not, I found myself fixating on the memory of one occasion when Bruce said to me that he did not want to be here and that he did not feel he belonged. I remember that he had been drinking at the time so I just thought that it was the drink talking. However, whether this was fuelled by alcohol or not, the weight of this knowledge along with many thoughts and questions hit me like a ton of bricks.

Why had I not done something earlier when he was an angry teenager?

Answer: I just thought it was teenage behaviour. On hindsight and if it were nowadays I would possibly seek professional advice to obtain a diagnosis of bi-polar or depression or seek help for anger management.

Why had I not brought him home from his father's house?

Answer: I truly believed he would be treated and loved as an only child. But knowing his father, I should have brought him back home to me and his siblings. I should have been the adult and protected my boy.

Why had I not talked more to him about how he felt?

Answer: I did talk to him and I tried to get him to realise that his consultation with professionals seemed to be more about getting academic or professional viewpoints on mental health than attending for his own mental health.

'You can take a horse to water but can't force it to drink.'

I did talk to Bruce about his drinking. I tried to tell him how it affected him and others. But he knew that and still didn't stop (until the year or so before his decision to take his own life). So one must realise that there is only so much another can do, but ultimately only the individual can be the one to take action to change.

Why had I not taken more steps to help him when he voiced his thoughts of not feeling he belonged?

Answer: At the time I truly thought it was the drink talking and, in some way, I knew what he meant when he said that he did not feel that he belonged in this world. Like me he was a sensitive, caring soul and neither of us liked the direction the world is going with more hatred than love for our fellow human beings. Bruce never liked reading about tragic events, being unable to bear the pain and suffering of the people involved.

I am able (not always of course) to put matters into perspective. Bruce found that difficult; he was always thinking of others. He constantly questioned: how could awful things happen to those around him and across the world? How could he help?

He was keen to become a journalistic photographer and had looked into various universities that offered photojournalism courses just months before his suicide. He was so excited about this prospect. However, after his death I spoke to his mentor, Martin Gilfeather who told me that Bruce could not have coped with the suffering that he would have seen in war zones. In any event it was never to be but I do have all his wonderful photography to remind me of his talent.

When Bruce told me he did not feel that he belonged in this world he did not specifically talk about suicide but when I now recall his words I get angry and guilty for not doing something about it at the time.

If only…hindsight is a great thing!

Could I have stopped him from taking his own life?

Answer: I do not really have an answer to this question. Knowing now through his letter (Appendix I) the pain he was suffering I think if I had stopped him, he would have been angry and even more determined to take his own life.

Since coming back home and seeing his anger and pain, his drinking and smoking I was constantly on edge when he went out. I wondered whether he would come home or if something would happen to him: would he be attacked? There was an ever-present nervousness in the air.

This might not be what people want to hear and it is painful for me to voice this here but I think it will help to share the following thoughts.

Knowing he is at peace, I am at peace. I no longer need to worry about him.

The questions I posed above are difficult and even impossible to answer properly given that we will never have the full story, but I have given my answers. They may not be the right ones but they are my honest answers and I hope in some way by raising these questions and giving my answers that they help someone who is in a similar situation.

I have tried to paint a picture of my boy Bruce (warts and all) but it is impossible to include every detail covering more than three decades of his life in just one chapter.

Writing about him has been cathartic and therapeutic for me. But it has also been emotional especially writing about his problems. I do still have times when I look back and wonder if I could have done something differently. Such thoughts invade my mind and I know they will continue to do so throughout my life. One thing that helps me, and hopefully helps others is this:

Remind yourself that there is no university or course that prepares you for parenthood. You do the best you can with the tools (and circumstances) you have at the time.

Bruce was my first born. I loved him from the moment I held him in my arms, just as I did my other three children. I thought Bruce would always know this but from our many conversations later in his life I am not sure that he did. He would say that if he ever had a child he would give all his love to that one child. However, that was not to be and I had three more children born each following year so he became the eldest.

One piece of advice I can give every parent is to tell your children that you love them but more than that, show it by your actions. I know Bruce is no longer with me but I find myself speaking to him and telling him that I love him.

Thoughts of not telling him how much he meant to me brings back a memory of long ago. This might resonate with some readers. I get very upset and find tears rolling down my cheeks when I recall one (or possibly more instances) of saying to Bruce—aged a mere two or three years old—when he maybe wanted to be carried: *'For goodness sake, you don't need carried, you can walk, you are the oldest, you're a big boy'* and similar such situations. So he had to grow up quickly or I made him grow up quickly. I watch parents who have one child and they are sometimes treated like 'babies' for some years and certainly past three years old.

If only.......oh how I wish I could take back some words!

I do have that feeling 'Oh how I wish...' But again I remember that having children was not really discussed when I got married. We just had children! In fact not having a particularly 'loving' childhood myself (and that is for another book) and realising on hindsight that I perhaps should not have married my ex-husband, I decided to make the best of the situation. I knew I wanted my own children that I could love, so that's what happened: I had four gorgeous children and wouldn't have it any other way.

I have already talked about the words from Bruce that were the deciding factor on making the decision to leave. These words will be with me forever.

'Mummy we have to leave……we have to leave'.

Prior to this I had on many occasions asked my ex-husband if he would let me go and I had hoped that with a successful business he would be fair and divide the share of the business so that we would all have enough to live on. I knew I could work so I was only interested in him paying for our children. This again was not to be. It took some ten years in the courts to finally get too little too late. This whole period of ten years impacted on myself and the children, more than I could ever imagine at the time. It clearly impacted on Bruce and I believe went some way (if not all) to his decision to take his own life.

Bruce's siblings seemed to cope with behaviour of their father and the contentious separation period but this does not mean that it did not affect them. I know it did and perhaps I should have talked to them more openly but again there is always a fear of raising difficulties and as I said before I am not good in confrontational situations. I know that Bruce's siblings were affected by the long period of the divorce. I know they have been and continue to be affected by Bruce's suicide. From the outset I was determined to talk about Bruce to his siblings and his nieces and nephews. His nieces and nephews drew pictures and wrote poems about him to be laid to rest with him and this made them feel part of his celebration of life.

There may have been many turning points in Bruce's life that led to his fatal decision to take his own life. For me it was his little voice telling me *'we have to leave…..'*

Another crucial turning point I believe was his decision to go to live with his father. As I said before, in my mind at the time, I believed that it might be a good decision as I believed (at least hoped) that he would be treated (and hopefully loved) as an 'only' child. It turned out that this was the worst decision he (and I) ever made. I believe that this scarred Bruce and, in my opinion, was another contributing factor in him deciding to end his life. Despite me telling Bruce that the best form of revenge was to succeed in life and be happy, he just never seemed to be able to get over the way his father behaved and all he wanted was an apology which never came.

I did not realise just how bad it had been for Bruce. Once again these thoughts haunt me:

If only……if only I had gone and brought him home….

This is a huge regret and I live with this every day.

As I said earlier when I would go down to London to meet him, I could see that beneath the façade of his upbeat manner and smiles his life was not a bed of roses. It was not just the difficulty of getting acting jobs but that he needed permission from his father to access money.

It is difficult for me to talk about Bruce's faults. For me the worst fault I would say was Bruce's addiction to alcohol. It did not help that in order to live from one acting job to another he worked as a waiter in some of the best bars and restaurants in London and in LA. This meant that drink was always close by.

Fortunately Bruce was always aware of the importance of healthy eating and I believe the healthy eating reduced the effects of drinking and smoking. I think Bruce was more affected by what he saw around him in the bars and restaurants. He would tell me about high-functioning individuals who worked Monday to Friday but then engaged in recreational weekends of drinking, smoking and taking cocaine.

I believe in his mind Bruce felt that if they could do this then he could too as he was only drinking and smoking. But this was not so. There is research on addiction but no definitive answer, but I believe that there could be more. In fact, after Bruce's death I discovered a meditation in one of his notebooks called 'star breath' which is a meditation to help with addiction. I have used this to design a MindBites[24] (Appendix V) meditation called 'star breath'.

On the matter of addiction or the way Bruce believed that his brain worked differently from others, another question comes to mind:

> *Could I have asked pathology to do an autopsy to find out if there was such a gene or brain issue for Bruce?*

But time flies when you are involved in all the practicalities after a suicide and the moment has long since passed. Anyway, would I really have wanted it done? Then I wonder whether it would help someone in the future which would have made it worthwhile. That moment is gone but what is forever in my mind is the phone call.

The phone call

I will forever remember that phone call. Wednesday afternoon while I was in London I noticed there was a message on my mobile phone. It was from Bruce so I phoned him back.

He answered—now this was unusual as he never answered his phone. He sounded different somehow. He did not sound depressed, or flat, or excited but calm and positive. He asked if he could walk my beagle Fudge but I said that a student friend was walking her. Another moment of flashback:

What if I had let him walk Fudge, would things be different?

Would somehow letting him walk my dog have stopped him from making his tragic decision?

I will never know. He then asked if I was alright. I said I was and that I was working in London but would be home on Friday and I would see him then. He did not confirm this but went on to calmly and quietly tell me that everything was going to be OK and that I was not to worry. The call ended and I was left with what I can only call a 'funny' feeling in my stomach. I could not put my finger on it but I was concerned and decided that I would go to his flat when I got back home on Friday.

---

[24] MindBites meditations on various topics available on www.mindcircles.co.uk and www.stepsforsuccess.co.uk

Why did I not act on my gut feeling?

The simple answer is that I was in London and Bruce was phoning from some 400 miles away. I could of course have contacted one of his siblings but I didn't.

Would it have made a difference?

It might have stopped him then but the inevitable would have happened. As I said before, once Bruce put his mind to something there was no persuading him otherwise.

But as I promised myself when I returned on Friday evening I went to his flat. It was a gated property which I couldn't open directly. To compound matters, none of the door buzzers were working. I phoned Bruce on his mobile but there was no reply. I looked around outside and I saw a light on in his top floor flat. So I decided all was well and went home.

Throughout Saturday and Sunday, I went through the same process; phoning but getting no reply, going to his flat finding that the buzzers were still inoperable. However, when I went to the building on both Saturday and Sunday I noticed one of the top floor flat windows was open, so I told myself all was OK. I remembered later that Bruce was a meticulous planner and that he would have deliberately left his windows open to lessen the impact of heat which would affect his body. A gruesome but true thought: planning down to the last detail.

By Monday I was really worried. Unknown to Bruce I had a pitch to make for funding for (believe it or not) a mental health gadget that I had developed. I was not going to go but I phoned my close friend to ask if I should do the pitch or go to Bruce's flat. She told me to do the pitch as I never put myself first and this gadget would help many with mental health problems. So I decided to do the pitch.

Since that awful day I have asked myself over and over again: *'Should I have missed the pitch and gone to Bruce's flat?'* Another unanswered question. Something I regret but in light of what I discovered later that day it would probably have been too late to save Bruce.

With my mind and heart decidedly absent from the presentation I turned up without the actual gadget! Needless to say I did not get the funding!

I rushed back home and by the end of the afternoon I was extremely concerned about Bruce so I went to a neighbour who works as a safety consultant on the oil rigs. He and his partner saw how upset I was and asked me what I wanted them to do. I said, *'I want you to bring your tools and break Bruce's f......door down'.*

So all three of us went to Bruce's flat and again being gated property the gates were locked and none of the buzzers were working. My neighbour was not daunted by this and climbed over the gates, managed to obtain access to the internal door, opened the gates to let me in and we climbed to the top floor. He was ready to break the door down when he noticed that the door was slightly open. I moved to enter but he stopped me and said he would go in first. I heard him shout, *'Bruce, Bruce'.* It seemed like an eternity but minutes later he came out, put his arm round me and said, *I'm sorry Pat, but he is gone. Bruce is gone. He has hanged himself......*. He hesitated and holding me closer he said in a quiet, calming voice *'But he looks very peaceful'*.

I remember being in shock but also knowing I had to phone someone. I phoned his brother who screamed and dropped the phone. He must have driven at top speed because despite living a fair distance away he arrived shortly after. Someone, I don't know who, possibly my neighbour who had found Bruce, must have phoned the police as they arrived almost at the same time as my other son. Neighbours from other flats started to come out and I remember feeling the need to tell everyone: *'My son has committed suicide, my son has hanged himself, my son has committed suicide, my son has hanged himself'*.

My other son told me he had phoned and told my ex-husband.

Meanwhile my close friend Morfydd arrived and knowing that my ex-husband would probably arrive (which he did) she versed the police on the situation, namely that my ex-husband might try to take over, but the police were prepared. When my ex-husband arrived and went to push past the police told him no-one was being allowed through. The police were very calm and professional. My other son knew one of them and they gave permits for the cars which were parked outside. They told us that a private ambulance had been called and that Bruce would be taken to the mortuary.

The remainder of that night is a blur. I drove home followed by Morfydd who stayed with me that night. My other son had already phoned Bruce's sisters and I phoned my sister and other close friends.

I knew that practical matters would need to be dealt with and such matters are a blessing as organising them keeps you busy. I felt sorry for some of my own neighbours whom I felt the need to tell that my son had committed suicide.

I think the need to tell everyone, even strangers, that my son had committed suicide was because somehow it made it more real.

When anything practical has to be attended to I am the person you need as I am very organised. I take notes, make lists and arrangements but for this situation I dreaded such practical matters as, knowing my ex-husband, I believed that he would try to take over.

I knew I had to put thoughts of what my ex-husband might do aside so I bought a new notebook to set out all the arrangements from that moment until the celebration of Bruce's life.

Funerals and celebrations of life

I have attended many funerals and celebrations of life. I have helped others make arrangements but I knew doing so for my own child was going to be one of the most difficult, emotional times of my life.

I wanted no friction so I realised that I would have to put emotions aside as best I could and remain focused on Bruce and how he would want his life to be celebrated.

So, onto the practical matters and the feelings aroused by organising the celebration of Bruce's life.

CHAPTER FOUR

PRACTICAL MATTERS

My notebook!

You might be wondering what my notebook has to do with all this.

I had hoped to publish this book before Christmas 2019 but my 'thinking' stalled things as I had lost my notebook. My mis-placing of this notebook was like the 'straw that broke the camel's back'. They say that it is always the small things that create the biggest problems and stress. And so it was with this damned notebook.

Anyone who knows me will know that I get very frustrated if I lose things. I knew this notebook was in my flat. I trawled through all my notebooks (no mean feat as I have many) but no notebook was found.

By now you have probably guessed that I have a compulsion to collect all things stationery, particularly notebooks and diaries. Friends know this too and often gift me notebooks of all shapes and sizes.

After trawling through my own notebooks, I had to forage through Bruce's many notebooks. If I am a hoarder of all things stationery, Bruce was as well and he also collected books, articles, photographs and everything associated with his creative pursuits. If my flat had been larger I would have taken all his possessions but I realised this was not feasible. However, I did not want to let go of Bruce's possession immediately. Fortunately, his brother has a large double garage so when he cleared Bruce's flat, everything was stored there. More on this later.

After a week or two or more I took myself off to friends in Spain to continue and try to complete writing this book. However, I got side-tracked with visits to Cordoba and the surrounding areas of the Las Alpujarras in the Andalusian mountains. I was also helping my friends to get their beautiful house and grounds ready for viewings as they had decided to sell it—oh how I will miss this heavenly bolthole in Spain. The visit replenished my heart, mind and soul and when I returned, I decided to look through Bruce's notebooks again and lo and behold I found my notebook—so no excuses now—so I had what I needed to complete the book.

Visit to Bruce's flat

Before we actually cleared Bruce's flat there were other matters to attend to. On the day after Bruce's death I visited his flat with Morfydd. I just had to be there to touch, smell and see everything that had been dear to my son.

On entering the flat the first thing that was seen was a step ladder and piece of rope hanging from the skylight window. Although shocked it was almost funny, it was as if Bruce was telling me to laugh. I decided to remove the step ladder to the hallway as I did not want his siblings to see how it had been positioned.

Looking round there were signs of his meticulous planning of his last moments and tragic decision. He had cleaned everything, washed all his clothes and tidied up; everything was in order.

The letters

Turning to the coffee table I noticed that there were letters; one addressed to me (repeated below and also in Appendix I) and the others to his siblings. I opened and read mine and his words brought me some comfort. Dated 3rd May 2014 and time 13:51.

> *Dearest Mummy*
>
> *It's truly no-one's fault. I just wasn't a well bunny. There was <u>NO FOUL PLAY!</u>*
>
> *I've done the washing, cleaned up, weird kinda feels normal, just doing stuff, but anyways' Mummy, it's no-bodies fault really. I dunno, it's just that I was trapped in another character, ...I love R (my brother) dearly, so dearly and my sister (G) so much and my wee sister (K) so much too! Please keep my notebooks/artbooks for reference too.*
>
> *Look on the bright side, Dad can read my obituary – there the connection might be made at last!!*
>
> *But to you my dear I'm sorry so so sorry. But it's gonna rock where I'm going, Rock.*
>
> *Much love as always. Bruce xx*
>
> *P.S. you'll need John's number I can't work obviously......*
>
> *Mummy, He's the best! TELL HIM all the best with family and all.*
>
> *P.P.S. Darling, there's some cash for you. I owe nothing to anybody!*

His siblings were not aware that I had gone to Bruce's flat, but I wanted—no, needed—to be alone, to look around and just envelope myself in his 'smell'.

I decided to close the letter and let his siblings and myself find the letters when they came the next day.

Before I left his flat, I sat on his bed and just looked round, taking everything in, committing it to memory. His bed was made, all his books, tools, everything was in order! I left everything the way it was and went home.

Next day his brother and I went together to Bruce's flat. Just as I had looked around, so did his brother. He too was amazed at how it had been meticulously tidied and cleaned. Although I already knew they were there I pointed to the letters on the coffee table. Bruce had written to each of us except his father. His brother got upset and asked me what we would do about his father as there was no letter for him. I found myself saying that he could give his father the sculpture of the Ram's head, a symbol of their highland 'clan'.

Later I got annoyed with myself for suggesting this but when I explained my annoyance to my friend Morfydd she reminded me that I did not make this suggestion to appease my ex-husband but I did it for my son to relieve his pain.

Removal of Bruce's possessions from his flat

His brother and I then discussed arrangements for the removal of Bruce's possessions (of which he had many). Fortunately, his brother had friends who owned vans and the removal was arranged and carried out within a couple of days. I went to see the flat for the last time and asked if the attic had been cleared too. It had not. When we investigated the attic there seemed to be as much stuff up there as in the flat! Some items were quite large and I could not imagine Bruce putting these up there by himself. So, the friends had to return to remove the possessions from the attic. Finally, the flat was empty leaving no evidence that Bruce had ever lived there. I was so sad and had to keep reminding myself that Bruce and everything he stood for was in my heart and memory for ever.

Not everything was stored in my younger son's double garage as I knew I had to keep Bruce's promise of keeping his notebooks and artworks safe. I took his books, notebooks, articles, magazines and artworks to my flat. The large, heavy photographic lighting equipment was donated to his college for the benefit of other students.

The obituary?

The days following Bruce's death were filled with various visits. One visit was to my ex-husband's house where he had demanded everyone attend including me! I had never been inside his house, so it was with trepidation that I entered. Apparently, he wanted us all there to 'speed the process' up by deciding on a 'collaborative' obituary for the newspaper. I knew Bruce would never have wanted this but he was gone and had left no instructions!

So, I attended the 'summons'. I was stunned, it was like stepping into our old matrimonial home and that was just the hall. I was led into the kitchen which was nothing like our old matrimonial home. Despite being told that a fortune had been spent on this kitchen it felt oppressive to me with too many cupboards, central unit, dining table and chairs and all made of what appeared to me as mid-to dark wood. The chairs round the table had all been taken by my ex-husband, Bruce's siblings, my wee sister and me. Although the reason for the meeting was to discuss an obituary, my ex-husband had already prepared it and passed it round for us to read. Bruce's little sister was horrified and said it sounded like the obituary for an old man. We all agreed but instead of arguing and presuming (incorrectly as it turned out) that my ex-husband was going to pay for the obituary I decided to say that an obituary in this particular tabloid can be expensive; cost being per line/word and so on. This did not elicit any response from my ex-husband. To bring the meeting to a close—it was getting awkward as always happened when my ex-husband was involved—I asked him to go ahead with his plan, knowing that any payment would probably fall on me or my children. We all left. The obituary was published in the newspaper on 13th May.

In my opinion my ex-husband wanted to arrange things so that he could take control. I was determined that this should not happen as I knew Bruce would not want this. If anything Bruce would have wanted as little fuss as possible.

I silently promised Bruce that I would do my best to organise his celebration of life in the way he would have wanted.

Attendance at the mortuary

The police had told me that as it was a sudden death at home a report would be sent to the Procurator Fiscal but that did not mean that they would take any action or delay my viewing of the body. As it turned out there was no delay and I telephoned the mortuary on 7th May to find out when I could see Bruce. The pathologist was very kind and told me how the process of viewing was done. She emphasised that it was not a 'viewing' but a formal identification and I was allowed half an hour to first identify my son and then sit with him. She advised me that there were no time slots available that day but she had various slots available on 8th May and I chose 9 a.m.

I phoned Bruce's brother and asked if he would go with me to the mortuary and he agreed to come along. I told him to contact his father and tell him to make his own arrangements if he wanted to do so and it later transpired that he had chosen 2 p.m. on the same day I was going and had asked Bruce's sister to take him. As it turned out he did want Bruce's brother to go with him; more on that later.

I asked Morfydd to go with me to the mortuary and we arrived at 7 a.m. sharp. My son met us there but Morfydd stayed outside.

We were taken to a small waiting room, which was tastefully furnished. It was peaceful and had an air of calm, yet it did not calm me or my son. We were both agitated as we did not know what to expect. I needed to see Bruce, yet I did not want to be there.

A young pathology assistant came in and explained the process. She told us that next door was the viewing room and it was divided into two with a glass partition and a curtain down the middle. When we entered, we could take a moment to settle ourselves and then when we were ready, we could go through into the other side of the room where Bruce lay on a bed covered with blankets. She asked us not to disturb the blankets (for obvious reasons!). She explained that he would feel cold, but we could touch or kiss him. She reminded us of the time limit, that we only had one half hour to do this. She then walked us through to the room and we saw the glass-curtained partition which divided the room between a seating area and where Bruce lay.

My son and I sat down on the chairs that were there—I wanted to go in, yet I didn't want to go in. I was desperate to see Bruce, but I did not want to see him under these circumstances. I didn't know what to do. My son was the same. We steeled ourselves to move and as time was short and precious, with determination and some trepidation we entered the other side of the partition.

It was not as I expected. Bruce lay on a bed with a blanket covering him. He looked as peaceful as if he was just sleeping.

My last kiss and goodbye

There was a chair nearby and I pulled it up to the bedside. He looked so peaceful I just kept repeating that I loved him. My other son was distraught and just kept saying *'you stupid b......why, why?'* I leaned over and touched Bruce's face: yes it was cold but he looked at peace. I wanted to stay with him for a long while, forever. I knew I had to let him go. Just as I was thinking this, and I can't explain it but hope many will understand, I felt a light breath leave his body that I believe was his soul leaving his body. It was like a physical act of the soul leaving. In my heart I knew then that this was him giving me permission to let him go. I sat for a moment more and my son stood beside me. We said our goodbyes and that we loved him and we left the room.

Only when I was in the other room and the assistant asked if we were ready to leave, I realised that I was not. I wanted to go back in and see him again. I knew this feeling would always be with me so we left, having first said our goodbyes and letting him go with love and peace.

What funeral directors?

Outside the hospital I asked my son what we were going to do about funeral directors as I believed that my ex-husband might want to make the decision without consulting us. My son told me there is one way to resolve this and he produced a copy of the local Yellow Pages book and flicked through to funeral directors. Closing his eyes, he ran his finger down the list and stopped at one. This is who we will use he said. The funeral directors turned out to be a small family business. I do like supporting family businesses and it turned out that they were professional as well as being helpful, understanding and sympathetic.

Once we agreed on the funeral directors, my son arranged for us all, including my ex-husband, to meet at their offices. At the last minute my son was unable to attend having been called out of town on business. However, he was happy with whatever decision was made about the funeral.

I met with Bruce's sisters and their father at the offices of the funeral directors. The office was small and I sat with my daughter on one side and my other daughter and my ex-husband (father of Bruce and my other three children) sat across from us. The funeral director explained the funeral process. I told them that Bruce would have wanted something simple. They understood the role of the Procurator Fiscal but if there were no issues then a certificate of death could be issued which would be taken to the Registrar.

They advised that the extra expense of medical certificates would not be required as Bruce had been taken to the mortuary. The cost of the funeral would be kept to a minimum and Bruce's siblings said that the cost could be shared.

Cars or not?

The funeral directors asked if we wanted cars and I declined, as did Bruce's sisters because both my son and daughters had black cars and there was more than enough space to take people to the crematorium. However, my ex-husband decided he wanted a car. My daughter asked him why and this caused upset. They both flew out of the office banging the glass door. I was worried that it would shatter but the funeral director laughed and said that the door had been broken on more than one occasion and that funeral arrangements often brought out the worst in people. In addition to this there was a pub on one side and a job centre on the other so there were often noisy arguments!

When my ex-husband and my daughter returned, as always I tried to make peace and started to say that their father was just thinking about us all. However this did not resolve the matter so I stopped talking or trying to bring peace to the situation. Eventually it was agreed that my ex-husband could have one car but that would be paid for by him. However, when I received the invoice from the funeral directors it included the car!

We then discussed who would be pall bearers—who would carry the coffin—and it was agreed that my son and Bruce's friend and colleague Johnny would do this. There was a pause and I can't really remember how this came about but to give their father his place he was given a position of pall bearer too. Knowing Bruce's feelings about his father I did not want him to be one of the pall bearers but decided to let that decision go through.

Bruce's siblings and I had a private laugh when we imagined their father being one of the pall bearers as there was a huge difference in height between him and the others carrying the coffin. We just imagined the coffin tilting as it was carried in!

We agreed that there would only be family flowers. I had hoped to set up a Bruce Foundation, a charity for mental health but this caused another quarrel so I left this idea alone to think about later.

The funeral director then produced a contract which I signed. My ex-husband had the opportunity at that time to also sign but he did not do so. The result was that the contract was between me and the funeral directors. This turned out to be to my advantage as when my ex-husband contacted them to tell them what to do they advised him that they could only deal with me as he was not part of the contract.

Visiting the police station

Bruce's belongings had to be collected from the police station. When I arrived at the police station I was taken into a small room and the police officer explained that he had listed all Bruce's belonging on a form. He would bring the belongings through to the room and I would confirm that all the items on the list were there and would be handed to me. There were 22 items on the list. I went through Bruce's belongings, which included his clothes, watch, wallet and other small items and confirmed that there were only 21 items on the table. I kept asking about item number 22 on the list which lacked any description. The police officer asked if I really wanted that item. I thought it was an odd question so I said, "yes, I would like item 22". He seemed nervous and asked me again if I wanted item 22. Again, I said "yes". Eventually he said nervously and quietly that item 22 was the rope! I laughed nervously and said, "definitely not!"

I wondered why they had included any item 22 without any detail. But when dealing with many traumatic deaths the police maybe don't think it through and just list everything. However, they forget that for an individual, like me, this was just one traumatic death. There is no obvious intention to cause hurt, but it was difficult to hear about item 22. Those who know me will understand when I say I took it to be one of the black humour moments in this whole episode of my life. Bruce had a wicked sense of humour and I have this too. I have always tried to live by the motto 'Laughter is the best medicine'. Hard though this may be to understand I did find humour (black humour) in some moments during this tragic time.

I must emphasise that the police at the actual scene on the night of Bruce's death were very sympathetic and in any communication with the liaison officer I was advised that grief counselling was available. It was also comforting in some way that Bruce's brother knew one of the police officers who attended that night. Another humorous moment happened when Morfydd said she was worried about getting a parking ticket! I am sorry to say that I responded to her with some choice expletives! The police stepped in immediately and issued everyone who had a car with a 'police' permit allowing cars to be parked without fear of a ticket.

One matter that could have caused upset and hurt was the communication from the Procurator Fiscal's office. The tenor of their letter was that I was 'a victim of a crime'. I realised that this was merely a standard letter written from a template, but some individuals in the same situation as me could have been upset and even angry at receiving such a letter. My hope for the future is that in circumstances of a traumatic death more care is taken when sending letters to individuals who have lost a loved one.

Black humour moment!

I left the arrangements for Bruce's funeral—which I call the Celebration of his Life—in the capable hands of the funeral directors. Never having suffered such a loss before there were some things I did not realise were needed. The funeral director called me to ask what I would like Bruce to wear. I had not thought about this. I asked his brother and sisters what they thought he should wear and they all agreed it had to be his red 'Man U' (Manchester United) shirt with number 7 on the back. I duly took it from his belongings and gave it to the funeral director. He looked at me and asked, "Is that all you want him to wear?" I had to laugh as again I had not thought about other clothing and asked him what clothing would be needed. The funeral director said that he assumed that I would want Bruce fully dressed. If not, then it would just be the football shirt and a basic white gown! I certainly did not want that nor did I imagine that Bruce would want to be dressed that way or in an un-dressed state.

I took myself off to town to buy new clothes for the first time since he was a wee boy. This was a no mean feat as Bruce was very particular about his clothes. He never wanted designer gear but his clothes had to be 'just so' and it was this 'just so' that was daunting for me. Bruce was tall and very slim so he would need jeans. I phoned my son and asked what type of jeans I should buy. After going into a few shops, I found one that had the ideal pair of jeans. A male shop assistant came over and asked me what type of jeans and size I was looking for. When I told him, he said I would be best to bring my son in to try them on. I found myself saying that this would be difficult as he was dead. The assistant fell back in shock at this revelation. I quickly told him I had not intended to shock him, but I needed the jeans for 'dressing' my boy for his funeral. On reflection I wonder if I still had this need to tell everyone that my boy was dead. Doing this seemed to make it real. I still find myself telling people but not quite as frequently as the immediate aftermath.

At the shop, I also bought some underwear and socks, and armed with all the new clothes I took them to the funeral directors' offices. They were pleased and said that they would take great care in dressing Bruce.

Registering the death certificate

This was another difficult time. I had signed the contract with the funeral directors and I wanted to take care of all the arrangements for my son. However, I discovered that my ex-husband had picked up the death certificate and had planned to register it. I decided to go to the Registrar's office and sure enough my ex-husband was there. He would not let go of the certificate as, in my opinion, he wanted his name to appear on the registered certificate. This notion upset me but while we were waiting to be seen by the Registrar, I decided to try to make peace and talk about the loss of 'our' son. Unfortunately, we couldn't resolve this disagreement. I had to let go of my upset and remind myself that the certificate was only a piece of paper.

Bruce's nieces and nephews

During the days of running about attending to practical matters, Bruce's brother and sisters told their children that their Uncle Bruce had passed away. They were all young and it seemed fitting not to go into detail surrounding Bruce's death. There was much crying but also lots of activity about what they could do. They wrote special cards with messages and drew pictures for Bruce. These were beautiful and were placed inside Bruce's coffin. Bruce loved to give me sunflowers so I placed one sunflower inside the coffin to go with him on his journey to 'where he would rock!'

The teddy

One item I could not let go of was a very small teddy wearing a scarf of another favourite football team of Bruce, Partick Thistle. I found the teddy on Bruce's bed in his flat when I visited the day after his tragic decision. In fact, the circumstances surrounding this little teddy are interesting. When I visited the flat with Morfydd the day after Bruce's death this little teddy was not on his bed! However, when I visited the flat following day with his brother, the teddy was sitting on the bed! No-one had been in the flat between my first and second visit. There are things that cannot be explained. I know some may or will not understand but I believe that Bruce was telling me, 'I'm OK. Take my teddy and let him comfort you when you need it'. This little teddy now sits on my bed and whenever I need a hug from Bruce I give the teddy a hug.

What date for Celebration of Bruce's life?

One cause for a near quarrel was that I wanted to wait for short time before the Celebration of Life could take place. The funeral directors said that there was no need to rush to do this within a day or two or even a week. My reason for waiting was that I needed time to contact Bruce's friends and colleagues and the lives he had touched wherever he had lived and worked, whether in the UK, the USA or further afield. I dug my heels in. As I said before Bruce and I had that same stubborn streak. So, although Bruce died on 5th May the Celebration of his Life was set to take place on 20th May.

Bruce was not religious but he had a spiritual, holistic mind so I knew he would be more than happy to have a humanist carry out the celebration. I knew the celebrant Jane Patmore as she had been the celebrant at the wedding of some friends, where Bruce had been employed as the wedding photographer; a unique decision for him as Bruce did not 'do' wedding photography. However, the bride for this wedding was arty and quirky and did not want the usual type wedding photographs and knowing Bruce and his photography she persuaded him to take the photographs at her wedding. I telephoned Jane and asked if she would be celebrant for Bruce. Before I could add that it was his funeral she asked if he was getting married and I broke the awful news that I wanted her to be the celebrant at his funeral. She was so sad to hear this but she was delighted and honoured to be celebrant.

I explained to Jane some of the difficult relationship background between Bruce, his siblings and their father. I also explained that I could not discuss my gorgeous boy Bruce in front of my ex-husband. I arranged for her to come to my home where we discussed Bruce. She also explained that she had planned to meet with my ex-husband and Bruce's siblings that night.

Later that night I got a phone call from my son to say that the meeting with Jane Patmore had been excruciatingly embarrassing. He said that Jane tried to give their father his place by asking him about his son, Bruce. Silence followed silence; their father said nothing. The silences were awkward and embarrassing and my son decided to jump in with stories of Bruce and the family and my daughters started to share their memories too.

What music?

More difficulties arose when we tried to agree on the music for the funeral. My ex-husband wanted traditional hymns: something Bruce would not want and fortunately neither did his siblings who knew what he liked. It was decided that they would choose music that Bruce loved. His brother arranged for a piper to play outside the crematorium. Inside the crematorium the introductory music was Serenade in C Minor by Mozart, a favourite of mine too. Once again to keep the peace, Bruce's siblings and I agreed that there could be one hymn and that was *The Lord is my Shepherd* played to the tune Crimond. The final farewell music was very special and summed up where Bruce was going and I knew he would be at peace:

> *I can see clearly now, the rain has gone*
> *I can see all obstacles in my way*
> *Gone are the dark clouds that had me blind*
> *It's gonna be a bright, bright sun-shining day...*

A CD was made of all the music and given to the funeral directors who would arrange to have it played at appropriate time. Of course, I have the CD which I can play at any time.

Where to hold the 'after' celebration gathering?

Yet another difficult decision. This time it started with me. Bruce had become friendly with people in the local pub and I thought it would be a good idea to hold the gathering there. I know that this pub had donated money towards Bruce's funeral and they were very happy to hold the celebration gathering for Bruce. However, after much discussion with Bruce's siblings I saw their point of view. I had to remember that Bruce was loved by many people from all walks of life and all ages. Some would live close, but others were coming from afar. There would also be friends of the family coming to pay their respects. So we all came to an agreement and I was pleased with the decision that the gathering after the funeral would be held in the local cricket and rugby club near where I lived with my four children and where they had many hours of fun. Bruce's sister (G) knew the owners and made arrangements for the gathering.

Bruce's photographs

I decided that everyone should see some of the talented photography taken by Bruce so I roped in my good friend Walter to compile a video of some of Bruce's work which could be played during the wake. This turned out to be a good decision as some people there did not realise that Bruce had travelled far and wide and had taken photos of the places he visited.

All these practical matters help the days go by leaving little or no time for tears. Some may resonate with this, but I think I went into robotic mode.

Another black humour moment!

I recall that visitors dropped in. Neighbours dropped in. Passers-by would stop and give their condolences. The humorous moment came when my regular postie who was used to delivering my letters began delivering flowers: bouquets, plants, some large, some small and lots of them. One morning he said to me, "Are you getting married?". Sadly, I told him no and that my son had died. He was so sorry to hear this and when I told him that Bruce had committed suicide he went on to share that over the last two years in the Post Office a number of young males had committed suicide. I told him when I had openly shared the news of Bruce's suicide, many people contacted me to share their stories of suicide in the family, at work and among friends. I knew and still know that there is a need to open up about suicides. I hope that this book will help to raise awareness and that the stories shared here will help others in a similar situation to know that they are not alone and hope that it brings some comfort and hope too.

Celebration of Bruce's life

I wanted to let all Bruce's friends know what had happened and invite them to the celebration. Sharing it openly on social media helped with finding some of his friends. However, the main challenge was that Bruce, like most young people, did not have a hard copy address book. Of course, he kept details of names and addresses on his phone but that was password protected. His social media was password protected. In fact, Bruce was obsessed with protecting everything. He even used black tape to cover over the brand names of this photographic equipment. He would not wear an expensive watch when travelling and said that he preferred to mingle with the locals. Of course, that was a sensible idea and his ability to speak with anyone led him to make friends with locals and he was often asked to stay, such as when he visited Cuba. I managed to make contact with his friends but it was too far for them to travel.

Fortunately, the power of the internet helped send the message far and wide and many people contacted me to say how shocked and saddened they were to hear the news. From speaking with his close friends nearly all said they had no idea that Bruce would ever consider suicide. Bruce had the ability to capture everyone with his smile and enthral with his wit, mimicry and talent for different accents. No-one really knew what lay behind that smile and I must say with regret that I did not realise the extent of his angst which only came to light when going through his notebooks and artwork after his death.

In addition to the welcome address by the celebrant, Jane Patmore and despite being told that I would not be able to speak about Bruce at his celebration of life I was determined to do so. And I did, speaking with pride. I have provided my words (Appendix III) and those of Jane Patmore (Appendix II) at the end of this book.

I was comforted by my daughter when we entered the crematorium as she reminded me of my own technique— 'red door/blue door'—which keeps tears in check when there is a need to do so. I share this tip later in the book. Bruce's brother gave an emotional but uplifting speech about his brother recalling many of the antics they got up to when they were younger (some of which I had either forgotten or did not know about!) Bruce's sister decided she would like to give a short speech too and Bruce would have been proud of her. My youngest was very distraught and did not give a speech and became even more upset about not doing so when her brother and sister had. However, Bruce would have been in no doubt that his brother and sisters all loved him dearly as he did them.

I must thank a good friend Margaret for compiling and printing the programme of Bruce's Celebration of Life, including heartfelt words:

> *Life is eternal*
>
> *Love is immortal… and death is only a horizon….and a horizon is nothing except the limit of our sight. Wherever a beautiful soul has been there is a trail of beautiful memories.*

The day of the celebration of Bruce's life

Although I had decided to leave some time between Bruce's death and the day of the celebration it came around quite quickly as I had been very busy with all the practical matters as I have referred to above.

Now it was here.

We had chosen the Johnny Nash song where there are words *'one day it's gonna be a bright (bright), bright (bright) sun-shiny day....'*. Well, Bruce had already arranged such a day for us. On waking that morning and for the rest of the day of his Celebration of Life it was indeed *'a bright, bright sun-shiny day.*

The skies were blue and the sun shone down brightly on us all.

It was all becoming very real.

To honour my beloved son, Bruce I had bought a new dress and jacket in navy blue, his favourite colour on me. When I wore or bought anything other than blue he would say, "Why are you wearing that colour, you suit blue best". When I tried it on in the shop and again when putting it on that day I could hear Bruce's voice whispering in my ear, "That's you, mum. I love you in blue".

Bruce's brother, sisters and I had arranged to meet in the morning at the local rugby club where the 'after' celebration gathering was to be held. This meant that we would all leave together and travel to the crematorium. Of course, the car that my ex-husband had organised was there too. We all made our way to the crematorium.

I had arranged for an artist's easel to be placed at the front of the crematorium hall. This showed a collage of all the photos of Bruce from babyhood to recent times.

I was overwhelmed by how many people had come to pay their respects. Bruce's friends from his school days, others from his time in London and many more of my friends and colleagues, as well as those of his brother and sisters.

We were ushered inside by the funeral directors and I had told them that I did not want to sit beside my ex-husband and they honoured my wishes. The coffin was carried in by the pall bearers and they then took their seats beside me. I noticed that Bruce's long-term friend carried a beautiful white rose which she later placed beside the family flowers.

The celebrant, Jane Patmore welcomed everyone and I know she spoke with depth and emotion about Bruce, having spoken with his brother and sisters and gathered lots of stories from his childhood and their love for each other. I really only know this from having read her 'gathering and welcome' after the funeral as like any emotional gathering I think it is impossible to concentrate on what is being said. In addition to this I knew I was going to talk about my gorgeous son and wanted to be as composed as possible. I am so glad that Jane gave me her full address as a memento and I have repeated it in this book (Appendix II).

When it was Bruce's brother and sister's turn to speak about him I nearly lost my composure. Despite it being such an emotional time for them they spoke calmly and with deep respect and love. I was so proud of them. A touching moment was when Bruce's brother moved over to the coffin and just bowed his head and touched it to say goodbye.

Then it was my turn. There was concern that I would not be able to do this but I was determined and my bloody-minded gene kicked in and there I was standing on the small platform facing all these wonderful people who had come to remember Bruce.

I managed to retain my composure as I talked about Bruce. However, at one point one of the photos fell from the collage and I remarked that this was Bruce telling me to 'cut it short'! I have included what I said in Appendix III at the end of this book.

Just as I stepped down from the platform a white feather fell from the ceiling. Another sign that Bruce was telling me everything would be OK. I felt the need to do as Bruce's brother had done and I moved towards the coffin. The falling of the white feather had unnerved me but I managed to touch the coffin just as I felt my legs buckle slightly. Bruce's brother swiftly came to my side and led me back to my seat. I felt for Bruce's youngest sister who was distraught but her brother curled his arm around her in comfort. I know she felt she had let Bruce down by not speaking about him as his brother and sister had done but there is no need as I know Bruce would understand and that she loved him dearly.

We did not stand and shake everyone's hand but moved outside. There was a sea of faces but I recognised a colleague who had travelled from Ireland and went over to him to thank him. I noticed others and some colleagues from Ayrshire came over to me and said I had done well and Bruce would be proud of me.

Everyone was invited back to the rugby club to continue to celebrate Bruce's life. I was glad that many came as it gave me and everyone time to chat and see the video of Bruce's photography which we had arranged to be shown. The gathering at the rugby club was anything but a solemn affair which Bruce would have abhorred. Rather it was upbeat and happy with much sharing of stories and laughter. There was a sumptuous buffet provided by the rugby club and drinks available for everyone. It was a beautiful end to a very emotional day.

However, the day did not end for me as I had decided to go with a few close friends to the local pub where initially I had intended for the gathering after the funeral to take place. When it was decided that the gathering was to take place at the local rugby club (and on hindsight that was the best decision) I warned the pub that the family had decided on another venue so they would not be put to unnecessary trouble and expense.

When we arrived at the pub they were very pleased to see us. They told us that they had 'raised a glass' for Bruce. We sat and had a few drinks. The manager came over and handed me an envelope. He said that all the regulars had clubbed together and donated money that they wanted me to have in memory of Bruce.

Suddenly I realised that 'it' was over and it was time to go home.

I opened the door and the tears just flowed.

Bruce's teddy & me

CHAPTER FIVE

AFTER MY LOSS

Immediate days

I did not really have time to think after the funeral as I had decided to carry out my tutoring duties at the Open University Residential Summer school. I knew this was the right thing to do for me as I was kept busy. Others may decide to take time off work or just sit at home but that was not an option for me. The residential school was starting in July so I still had a few weeks in which to carry out other practical matters.

As I said in the previous chapter, I had already picked up Bruce's belongings from the police station and I had his teddy from my visit to his flat. I found myself smelling his clothes, clutching his teddy, and letting the emotions flow through my body until I could almost feel him beside.

I found it very difficult to get rid of any of his belongings. I still have his clothes folded neatly in a drawer in my flat. I still find myself opening this drawer and breathing in 'his' smell. I have his academic folders and his photography and artwork notebooks. They too have his distinctive smell. This is my Bruce. I let my lungs fill with the aroma. I can't really describe the aroma but it is unique to my Bruce and it's mine.

The ashes

I received a call from the funeral directors to let me know that Bruce's ashes were ready to collect. I had already agreed on the container for the ashes. There are so many types now; from silver urns to large cardboard tubes which have different nature scenes on them. I agreed on one large tube with beautiful sunset scene and three smaller silver urns. One was for me and one for his long-term friend who was taking them to Denmark where she would create a small garden for Bruce.

Bruce's garden in Denmark

The third one was for me to scatter his ashes in London and other parts of the world where Bruce had been. His brother scattered ashes in the Pacific Ocean beside Venice Beach in California where Bruce had spent many happy years as an actor.

Bruce's brother scattering ashes in the Pacific Ocean, Venice Beach, California

Although Bruce's nieces and nephews had not attended the funeral as they were too young, it was decided that we should all meet up and scatter his ashes in a favourite nature spot where he had often walked with his sister.

Yet another black humour moment!

Although I have arranged and attended funerals I had not been involved in picking up or scattering ashes. I was quite astounded when I picked up the ashes from the funeral directors' offices: the ashes filled not only the large tube but also three silver urns with another two boxes! Although Bruce stood at 6-feet tall he was very lean and I never thought he would fill so many boxes!

The large volume of ashes meant that I had enough for many scatterings around the world as well as having some available for making a gorgeous silver–blue pendant, silver–blue ear-rings, blue spiral paperweight and silver–blue ring. These are made by Ashes into Glass[25] and now Bruce goes with me everywhere.

Having emptied Bruce's flat, I now had his books, notebooks, photographs and pictures/artwork brought to my house. I wanted to read his notebooks, yet I didn't for fear of what I might read. I knew he had dark moments throughout his life and being an avid reader and writer I believed that he would have written about these moments in his notebooks. This turned out to be true as I read some of his notebooks. Like me, he starts one notebook, stops, starts another, stops, goes back to the first one and so on. Exactly what I do. We are like two peas in a pod.

I also found myself not wanting to share what he had written with any family members. I think I just wanted to keep him to myself. Keep things private. Knowing how he was such a private person.

Perhaps it is not what others would do, but I did want to be alone. I needed time alone. Others felt they wanted to be with me which was very kind of them but I just wanted to say, 'you can go, I want to be alone'.

Naturally there are people who avoid you at all costs. These are the people who, when they see you, cross the road or turn down a different supermarket aisle to avoid speaking with you or even making eye contact. I didn't get angry or upset by these people as I know it is always difficult to know what to say when someone has lost a child or loved one, no matter the circumstances.

However when I did bump into people and I could see by their faces and eyes that they were anxious and nervous about saying the right thing I would always make the first move and say, "It's OK to talk about Bruce. I am OK. I want him to be remembered so don't worry about saying his name."

Weeks following

The few weeks after the funeral passed quickly as I was preparing for the Open University residential school. This was a blessing for me as, having done this for many years, I always enjoyed my time with colleagues and students at the residential schools. I did not tell anyone of my loss until I arrived. All my colleagues were concerned and asked if I was sure that I was OK. I assured them that I wanted to be there. I also knew that I had their support if needed.

Every year, new students come to residential school and this was another blessing. I always give a talk at the residential school weeks and this was no exception. I decided that I would give my usual talk but open it with my news that my son had committed suicide. I told the audience that I did not make this announcement to shock but to raise awareness of suicide. My news was met with very positive feedback and I was approached by many who had suffered similar personal experience of such loss or had a family member or friend who had experienced this.

---

[25]   Ashes into Glass – tribute jewellery for a loss of a loved one www.ashesintoglass.com

I realised then that I had to not only talk about Bruce's suicide but also write about it. This has come to fruition with this book (albeit some five years later)!

I connected with many students on that residential school and I continue to keep in touch with my colleagues and many students whom I have taught.

Wherever I go, whether talking, lecturing or tutoring in different fields I talk about Bruce. By doing this I have discovered that there are many more suicides than we realise.

When I returned from Open University residential school that year I was contacted by various academic institutes offering me appointments as an examiner in procurement, law, ethics, personal development and associated topics.

I am self-employed with my own business MindCircles, which I started some years ago. My aim initially was to offer an online programme which could reduce stress and harassment while improving overall relationships within the workplace. I was fortunate that a large car manufacturing business took the programme on trial and it proved successful. Getting other industries on board proved challenging as I was usually met with the decision makers of companies telling me there was no need for such programmes as their employees were not stressed. This was despite being told by employees that there was stress, bullying and harassment in their workplace.

I made the decision then to concentrate on individuals and offer an online programme that would help them as individuals to cope with stress in all the challenges they faced in their lives.

This decision was not made lightly but it did mean a change of strategy and being online was going to be expensive, so when I received the calls to work as an examiner for various academic institutes I welcomed them with open arms.

When I was confirming these appointments, I recalled Bruce's words: 'Don't worry Mum, things will turn out all right…you'll be OK'. His words have turned out to be so true. In addition to examination work I have been asked to author various academic books and give inspirational talks all of which enables me to progress MindCircles and MindBites.

> *Bruce is definitely watching over me. But this does not make up for the fact that he is not with me in person, to hold and hug.*

At last I now see my dream coming true: bringing MindCircles[26], my MindBites[27] and my Steps for Success[28] online programme to the world.

---

[26]   MindCircles – www.mindcircles.co.uk
[27]   MindBites – shop at www.stepsforsuccess.co.uk
[28]   Steps for Success online program – www.stepsforsuccess.co.uk

Years following

It is almost six years now since Bruce committed suicide and I still find myself thinking that he is going to bounce in the door and start chatting. Sometimes when I hear a knock at the door or the letter box I think it is him. I don't think this feeling will ever go away.

I have his television with his trademark silver shape blocking out the brand name. Sometimes in the middle of the night it will turn itself on. Sometimes when it is on it shuts down as if to say, 'I'm here listen to me.' Crazy? Yes, it might be but then we would all like to think that our loved ones are around and do things to remind us that they are there if not in person, then in spirit.

Every year on the day of his celebration of life, 20th May, lots of white feathers fall from the sky into my garden. On other occasions I find a roll-up cigarette beside my back door, where he used to stand and smoke. As far as I can tell no-one in my complex smokes roll-ups. Whether they do or not I like to believe it is Bruce visiting me.

On the evening of the Celebration of his Life, a film producer friend took a photograph of the evening sky and he assured me it was not Photoshopped and there was an adult with his arm around a smaller person.

Sunset sky with clouds like two people (Courtesy of Charlie Francis)

All these unusual events, whether coincidences or not bring me comfort.

Bruce will live on in my heart and soul forever.

CHAPTER SIX

As time goes by

Dealing with loss over a month, years or many years remains an endurance test. I am fortunate that I seem able to see the positives which have come out of the Bruce's death. I had hoped to set up a Bruce Foundation and this was not to be. I still hope to raise money for a charity that deals with prevention of suicide and help those who have been affected by suicide.

Even after nearly six years I still feel the same. I still have days where something triggers my emotional pain and I can't stop crying. Usually it is music that does this but sometimes it can be at an unexpected moment when I see something that Bruce would have loved.

One such occasion arose when I climbed Sydney Bay Bridge, Australia. Bruce had never visited that country but knowing how much he loved photographing buildings and bridges when I reached the top of the bridge I made a video about Bruce in his memory. When I was leaving the Bay Bridge area I heard someone call out, "Bruce, Bruce." I turned and there was a chap walking behind me. In that split second, I thought it was Bruce, tall and lean, then I realised it was a stranger. But why the name, "Bruce, Bruce"?

On another occasion when I was on a plane to Melbourne there was a mother with a young son whom she was soothing as he had a cold. He had blonde hair and blue eyes just like my Bruce when he was a baby. I wanted it to be me all those years ago. I wanted my time over again. I was lost in thought when I heard the mother ask the flight attendant for some water for her son. The flights attendant asked her son's name and she said, "Bruce".

I have been on buses and trains and could have sworn that I saw Bruce. I even thought I'd talked to him. Some of you who have lost a loved one may understand this and have even experienced such moments. All I say is that you are not crazy. There are many things in this world that we cannot understand and that science cannot explain. To me, it does not matter, if it brings me comfort then I am happy that it is so.

Any incidents and moments like these that can help you endure everyday then accept them for what they are.

Dealing with my emotions

Grief

Grief differs depending on the loss or situation. It is also experienced differently by each individual. Remember that at some point in your life there will be at least one encounter with grief through the loss of a loved one, even the loss of your job, or break-up of a relationship. Grief is not restricted to loss through death. Therefore, it is important to be aware of what happens when you suffer loss.

I once wrote about the stages of grief. When I look back this was a naïve view of grief. It was only when I experienced the sudden death of my son, Bruce, to suicide that I realised what grief really meant.

However, it is useful to know that there are stages of grief. I can say that there are stages, but they do not appear in the same order. Sometimes they all appear in one day, even over the course of a single minute and you can find yourself dissolving, falling apart with tears rolling down your cheeks in torrents. I have some tips which I provide in Appendix V at the end on how to stem the flow of tears when it is inappropriate to cry so much that you fall apart. Don't get me wrong: you must not hold back the tears forever. Crying is a natural emotion and if denied can create further difficulties for you and lead to depression, or further depression if you have already been depressed.

Stages of grief?

For now I will give a brief overview of the stages of grief, some or all of which you may recognise if you have suffered loss. As I said above, this is not just through the death of a loved one but from other situations, such as a break-up of a relationship, even the loss of your job.

Grief does not follow any rules. You might not cry immediately because you are in shock. You might want to withdraw from everyone and everything you know which is difficult for those around you to understand. You might be angry. You might or will feel empty. No matter what you feel these are normal feelings for you as each person will experience grief differently. Some say that although we experience grief differently the order of the various stages is the same for everyone. I have not found this but then we are all different.

The first person to identify that there are stages of grief was Elizabeth Kubler-Ross (1969)[29] and she identified five stages, but these were related to people who were ill. However, they are the most well-known. There are others which include seven stages and another with two stages.

I vowed that this book would not become an academic book on grief so whether there are two, five or seven stages of grief I can only speak for myself and how I was affected by the sudden loss of my son to suicide.

In short, the five stages identified by Kubler-Ross were:

- Denial
- Anger

---

[29]   Kubler-Ross, Elizabeth (1969) *On Death and Dying – Kubler-Ross model of grief*

- Bargaining
- Depression
- Acceptance

Whatever the stages or order, grief is overwhelming. It can be intense and sudden. I wanted a title for this book which 'said it all' and I think the title '*The Weight of Emptiness*' does this.

Sometimes your grief is so intense that the emptiness inside you is heavy and it weighs you down so much so that you feel you cannot go on. At other times it creeps up on you but it might be at a time when you recall a happy memory and the weight is lighter, enough that you can cope. Then the tears might come in torrents running down your cheeks filling that emptiness that again you feel heavy. It is like being in a roller coaster that you cannot stop, you cannot get off, yet you maybe don't want it to stop, you don't want to get off as you might have to face reality and that your loved one is gone. We can explain it in the following way.

First stage of grief: denial. This is when you pretend that the loss or change has not happened. This feeling of pretending can lessen and even numb you to the intensity of the loss. I know Bruce is gone but I sometimes wait for him to come in the door; speaking so quickly about all the creative ideas that are invading his head. This is so real that I actually find myself thinking that it has happened. As quickly as this happens I realise that he is not going to rush in the door. Emptiness fills me and I have to focus on the fact that he is now at peace.

Second stage of grief: anger. The anger stage was identified by Kubler-Ross. I am not sure I have experienced intense anger but I do know that I have been angry at myself for not realising that Bruce was considering suicide. I know that his brother was angry when we visited the mortuary to say our goodbyes. I can hear his brother's voice now: "You stupid b..... you stupid b...........why did you not confide in us...." But not all people contemplating suicide will let others know of their plans. Indeed, someone said to me if only you had gone to his flat sooner. That phrase again 'if only......' Well what I do know of my son is that he would have been angry and would have found another time, another place. His letter to me (Appendix I) said it all.

Not everyone will experience feelings of anger, others might be angry for months, even years. They are stuck and repeatedly ask 'Why, why did they do this?' Being stuck in the angry stage for a long period can and will affect their mental and physical health as they are pushing other emotions aside. It is helpful if you are in that angry stage to seek professional help as you need to think rationally or be helped to think more rationally about your loss.

In one sense I am fortunate as I have no difficulty in talking (as many of you know) but I mean talking about Bruce. This helped me and writing this book helped me. I know from those who have shared their stories that by writing about their thoughts, feelings, words it has been therapeutic and helped them too.

Third stage of grief: the bargaining stage. This stage that Kubler-Ross identified refers to the 'what if' statements but in a different way: the 'what if' they mean is what if I do this then my pain will go away or I will be healed. Some people may turn to God or a higher power and make a bargain that if they pray more often or do some good deeds that they will heal and the pain will go away. This 'what if' stage is a way of trying to affect the outcome of an event, even a loss. The 'what if' stage is a way of postponing or delaying your hurt, confusion and sorrow.

When I look at what I have written I have referred often to the 'what if' so in a way I too have been experiencing the bargaining stage such as 'If only I had spent more time with my children'. However, for me the 'what if' is more about what I should have done before I lost Bruce and not how I can affect the outcome now. Bruce is gone and 'hindsight is a great thing!'

Fourth stage of grief: depression. Depression is the next stage identified by Kubler-Ross but as referred to earlier these stages are not necessarily experienced sequentially. They might be experienced all at one time. Depression, like grief, is different for everyone. No-one experiences depression in the same way or same intensity. Some people may not notice that you are depressed. When Bruce committed suicide it was at the same time that Robin Williams took his own life. Other actors and comedians have done so too. To the outside world they appear happy and upbeat. Underneath they are suffering from depression, so it is not unusual for people not to notice if someone is depressed. Bruce liked to read and would often refer to Stephen Fry and how he suffered from depression. Before he talked openly about this no-one would have guessed that he suffered from depression. Many others like him are very good at hiding how they feel.

People may isolate themselves or others may throw themselves into work; anything to keep the feelings of grief from being heavy and dragging you down. If you are aware that you are suffering from depression then you should seek professional help. However, this is not as easy as it sounds as often those suffering from depression are in denial. Even those around them will find it difficult, perhaps even impossible to get them to seek help from a mental health professional. Sometimes those in depression will use phrases such as 'What's the point of going on?' 'How can I go on without them?'

Fifth stage of grief: acceptance. Acceptance as identified by Kubler-Ross does not refer to someone finally being happy. It just means that they have accepted that their loved one has gone or the situation has changed. It does not mean that their grief is gone. Grief is with you forever but what changes is the way you view it.

When I lost Bruce I took comfort in his letter (Appendix I) to me and it gave me an insight into just how much pain he was suffering. When grief is too heavy I think on how he is now at peace and that he would want me to be happy. I am also grateful for having given birth to a wonderful, sensitive, creative boy and for all the memories of my time with him.

I think back on his last phone call with me when he said, "Don't' worry Mum, everything is going to be alright now." I did not realise then but since his death my business has grown in ways I could never have imagined. The tips and techniques for improved wellbeing which he helped me develop are now being recognised worldwide.

Other stages of grief?

Other stages that you might experience are feelings of disbelief or feeling numb or even the need to tell everyone. I remember when I was with my neighbour and friend who found Bruce, I heard myself telling everyone around me 'My son has committed suicide'. When I think back I am sure I was saying this to make it real. I didn't want to accept that he had gone and wanted to shout it from the roof tops.

With the pain of grief, what might come is intense pain. The loss is so unbearable that you want to take it out on everyone around you. I did not find this but I did have feelings of guilt about what I could have done while bringing him up or as I referred to earlier was it feelings of shame[30] that I was a bad person for not doing more. Back to that 'what if....' again.

Another stage which may come at different times for individuals but possibly much later (even years) is a feeling of calm or being calmer. I am not sure that this stage exists. At times I do feel calm but it comes and goes. Part of me doesn't want to feel calm. I want to remember the loss. However I have moved on in a different way, accepting that Bruce will not be back but that he would want me to move forward and I will always have the memories.

I have blogged for a number of years now through my MindCircles website[31] about various topics, from my personal experiences, how to feel good, my 7 Attributes, Resilience and Courage and other emotional issues. I have blogged about grief but since losing Bruce my views changed. However, even before that, my views changed when one very special friend had lost his first beloved granddaughter. In memory of their beautiful granddaughter they held a charity ball to raise money for the many medical professionals who attended her. They called this the Butterfly Ball. Shortly after my friend had suffered this loss I opened my computer to be confronted by a page where a mother was sharing the loss of her 13-month-old child she called 'her butterfly'. It was very courageous to share her experience but more than that it was not a depressing story but an inspirational one. She described how her child's life and sudden death had been the motivation to set up her website to share her emotions and feelings with others. When I opened that page to see the word 'butterfly' and a picture of a butterfly I believed that I was meant to write about the experience of death and grief.

Many people, often those closest to us, avoid asking questions about 'death' and 'loss' and it takes a stranger to innocently remark or ask questions about your loss or your feelings.

When you think you have had enough time to 'accept' what has happened and even when years have passed, you may welcome questions but there are times when, for some reason, such questions raise emotions in a big way and you miss the person as if the death had just happened and it is devastatingly heart-breaking.

To lose someone with whom you have a connection, whether that be a child or grown up, there will be many times, moments, every day that you miss the touch, voice, smile and 'smell'.

---

[30]   Lewis, Helen Block (1971) *Shame and Guilt* International University Press, New York

[31]   Blogs by Patricia Elliot – in books and continuing on www.mindcircles.co.uk

Remember grief is not a linear journey. The stages do not always come sequentially. All stages can be experienced in one day!

Lots of good may arise from a loss but this does not make it any less painful. Our society tends to want you to move on and that may be partially true, as replaying the past again and again many people would say is 'a waste of the present' but there will be many times your feelings are very strong, so strong and that is not the time to ignore them or put on the stiff upper lip.

Let yourself feel what is happening in that moment.

When I wrote a blog about my friend's loss I dedicated it to all the 'kids' and 'grown ups' who are sick or whom you have lost and for the very special nurses, doctors, consultants, carers who look after them.

I have repeatedly said in this book that sharing his healing. However, I know that all of us need more than just support. Of course if you find yourself not coping then you should seek help from professionals. I also believe that it can help to have tips, techniques and tools to help you with your grief and to move forward, albeit in a different way.

Tips for understanding grief

I know from speaking to others who have lost a loved one that people avoid them, some say people cross the road when they see them coming. Some say inappropriate words such as 'He lived a long life' or 'It was her time'. These words are said not to make you feel bad or unhappy but usually because they do not know what to say!

I found a way of dealing with others after I lost Bruce. When I met someone, whether that was a friend or just people who had heard of my loss I would immediately mention Bruce by name and tell them that it is OK to talk about him. I found it put people more at ease and comfortable with speaking about my loss.

Seeking professional help?

Of course if you need or someone you know needs help with coping with their loss then they should seek help from a mental health professional but you cannot force people to do this. You can suggest but it is up to them to take that step. Meanwhile if it is a close friend or family member then try to keep a watchful eye over them.

Remember that you cannot save everyone who decides to take their own life. Some people might try it as a cry for help. Others like Bruce made his decision and took time to write letters to me and his siblings. These were carefully worded letters which seemed to me that he had made his mind up and nothing would have stopped him.

This may sound odd to many but knowing that he is out of pain is of comfort to me. Also his 'lows' when he did not know what to do or how to behave had caused me unending worry. When he went out, wherever he went I worried about what might happen to him. Now my worries are over and I am at peace knowing he is safe.

The Weight of Emptiness will be with you always but it will vary in weight. I provide tips in Appendix V but when or if the 'weight' of grief gets too heavy or too much for you there are useful resources on depression and suicide which can be found by searching these words on the world wide web which will highlight appropriate websites and information for your particular area or country.

Life-threatening experience?

If what you are feeling or experiencing is life-threatening then you should call the appropriate emergency number (999 is the main emergency number for UK which should only be used when urgent attendance by emergency services is required). (112 is the same as 999 and it works on a mobile phone anywhere in the world. The EU requires that emergency call centres must provide translation services). Please check out these numbers as this information is provided as at the date of writing this book. Other numbers may or will be different for other countries and it is impossible to include all information here.

CHAPTER SEVEN

COMFORT AND HOPE

Resilience and endurance

Resilience and endurance are key to helping you get through difficult times. I also provide tips and tools (Appendix V) that I often use myself to help you in this process. I find them very helpful not just in difficult moments but also every day in that they bring me (and I hope you) comfort and hope. I sincerely ask you use them, practice them so that you increase your resilience and manage to endure each day in as positive a way as possible.

> *Remember your loss will be with you always but you can choose to take a different view of your loss*

I often hear people talk about being a survivor when they lose a loved one, but the word 'survivor' implies that you have overcome something. When a loved one dies whether by suicide or any other means I believe that you do not and will not overcome such a loss.

I know that I will never overcome the loss of my gorgeous son Bruce but rather I like to think of myself as enduring every moment of every day and it is a 'lifetime' endurance test.

For such endurance you need to look at what attributes you have. I describe seven in my *7 Attributes for Success (Inner Success and Happiness)* book[32]. The ones that are very appropriate for dealing with loss are the second (audacity/bravery/courage) and the third (resilience) attributes. My attributes are updated in my book Resilience and Courage: the key to endurance[33].

You need to be brave, be resilient and most of all think of the beloved child that you have lost. In my case, knowing that Bruce is at peace goes some way to helping me get through the difficult times. I also know that Bruce would want me to remember all the good times, the happy memories and for me to live my life so that his was not lived in vain. I sincerely hope that this book goes some way to doing this as well as helping others who have lost a loved one.

---

[32]   Elliot, Patricia (2010) *7 Attributes for Success (Inner Success and Happiness)* Authorhouse, available on <u>www.mindcircles.co.uk</u> and Amazon

[33]   Elliot, Patricia (2020) *Resilience and Courage: the Key to Endurance* Authorhouse, available on <u>www.mindcircles.co.uk</u> and Amazon

Remember of course that enduring does not mean that you don't cry. You will have moments (or days) where you just want to cry. This is OK—indeed it is needed (a must) to help you endure.

Some tips for enduring

Key to help in times of suffering from emotional pain are courage and resilience. Techniques that do help, if practised regularly, are effective (deep) breathing, relaxation meditations and mindfulness activities. The effective breathing techniques are particularly helpful for bringing about calm immediately. I developed MindBites[34] videos and audios which are short meditations to help in many situations from relaxation, to help you feel calm, energised, and focused, as well as being able to deal with anxiety, fear and anger.

My ABC stands for Affirmations, Breathing and Creative Visualisation which are psychologically proven techniques for improving overall wellbeing as well as helping you cope in the moment of and after traumatic situations as well as where you are experiencing acute stress.

I always try to provide easy to use techniques but do not be fooled: although they may be easy to use the hard part of the process is to use them regularly so that they become a good habit. It is easy to create bad habits, but not so easy to create good ones!

Situations where you may experience emotional pain are manifold and include loss, grief, stress, destructive relationships and trauma. It is necessary that you cope with your emotional pain in a healthy way. This will also help the healing process.

Although it is important to express your emotions and feelings, I described earlier how the emotional pain you feel can come at any time and it may not be appropriate or you may not want to cry or express your emotions at that time. I use a particular exercise that can help you in such a situation. I call this my red door/blue door exercise (Appendix V).

When you are experiencing emotional pain you can find yourself stuck, not able to move forward, overwhelmed by negative feelings. This is not healthy and will stop you from living your life to the full and unable to realise your true potential. If you have lost a loved one, as I have, then I am certain your loved one would not wish you to put your life on hold. They would want you to live a full life.

It is understandable that you might want to avoid your emotional pain or even not deal with the pain. However, by doing so you will only find yourself trapped and holding on to your negative feelings. You may turn to alcohol or other substances or even become addicted to shopping, eating and much more as a way to numb your pain. Avoiding or numbing your emotional pain by turning to alcohol or other substances or activities is only temporary and does not help you heal. I developed MindBites meditations to help you cope and I have one that helps you deal with addiction.

> *Remember: Avoiding or not dealing with your emotional pain can and will impact not only on your mental health but your physical health as well.*

---

[34]   MindBites meditation videos and audio available on www.mindcircles.co.uk and www.stepsforsuccess.co.uk

Unresolved grief or any emotional pain can result in you finding yourself experiencing even more periods of increased stress or anxiety later on. In addition to this you may find yourself suffering from physical symptoms, such as difficulty in sleeping or increased blood pressure.

I am sure that you would not want your emotional pain to impact on your mental or physical health and therefore it is vital that you deal with your emotional pain in a health way. You can do this by practising good coping skills so that they become a good habit.

Remember: taking care of yourself is also very important

Take your pain seriously

You are probably thinking what a ridiculous thing to say. However, in psychology the first step in the healing process is to 'honour your pain'. This means accepting that you are experiencing emotional pain and that something caused that pain. In my situation of suffering, the loss of my son to suicide, I can and do say to myself, 'I suffered the loss of my gorgeous son, Bruce and it hurts deeply. It doesn't matter what anyone else thinks; I hurt'.

If you have experienced emotional pain then you too can say something similar, such as, 'Something happened to me. It hurts...' and so on.

Emotional pain goes beyond just being sad. You feel the pain in the depths of your soul. You might meet people who tell you to 'get over it' or, 'it's been a long time now so you need to get on with your life'. I know these people do not mean to hurt you but they do not know what you are going through and if anyone has suffered the loss of a loved one then they will know that you do not get over it. You learn eventually to endure each day and each moment in a different way. It does not matter that you did not see the tragic event coming or not: you feel the same and you wonder why it happened. You are devastated and lost.

Remember that whatever has happened, even if the experiences seem similar, your pain and hurt is personal to you. When people tell you that they understand, they really don't. You might even resent them for saying this.

What can you do if you are a friend of someone who is experiencing emotional pain? The most effective way is to give them 'space'. Don't try to give advice or answer questions when they ask, 'How could this happen? Why did it happen?' Instead, be there and allow them the time to be alone with their thoughts. This can be difficult as you are probably desperate to fill the silence but just stay quiet and still.

It is also healthy to just sit by yourself and acknowledge your pain and your feelings. This is very difficult to do but it is a healthy way of dealing with grief and helps in the healing process. Sitting by yourself and acknowledging your feelings lets you be aware of how you are feeling in that present moment. It also gives you time to reflect and accept your feelings. It also gives you much needed time to cry.

Such moments alone also give you time to self-reflect. One of the stages of grief is anger, sometimes at yourself, sometimes at others. If you have experienced a tragic situation which is outside of your control, then it is important and helpful to look at how you deal with the situation. In my case I might get angry at Bruce for taking his own life. I sometimes get angry and feel guilty as to what I could have done differently.

If you have experienced pain through a situation where you were a victim, for example, a crime, then this can lead to a feeling of helplessness as you may not have had any control over the situation. You may still ask yourself whether you could have done something different and handled it in a different way. You might even berate yourself that had you gone home a different way, you might have avoided the attack. I suffered from an attack many years ago and I know that I did ask myself such questions. Even close friends asked me why I had taken that route home. Such questions are really the 'what if...'

Remember hindsight is a great thing!

What is important is to focus on what you learned from such an experience. Concentrate on what you can do in the future or how you can change things for the future. I was fortunate that I had a friend who told me to immediately walk that route again so that I would not be or continue to be afraid. I did so and although it seemed an odd thing to do at the time, I know it helped me to move forward. Fortunately, I subsequently moved to another town but what I did learn from the experience of the attack was to be cautious: always plan ahead where possible and be aware of your surroundings. Above all I focus on the positive.

I have faced many challenges in life, been knocked down by a few but never experienced such pain as the loss of Bruce. There are moments when I wanted to lie down and not get up. However, as you know, if you trip and fall, particularly in public, you have this immediate desire to get up and move (partly because you are embarrassed). Conversely, if you experience tragedy, no matter what, you should not try to 'get back up' immediately. Let your emotions and tears flow. Do not ignore the intense emotional pain. Just as ignoring serious physical pain can make matters worse, so too can ignoring emotional pain. First acknowledge it before you move forward positively.

Read on for some more tips which can help you do this.

Writing about your emotional pain

Writing about your emotional pain can be extremely therapeutic. Those who have shared with me their stories of loss have told me that writing their experience has helped them and brought some comfort. I know that sharing their stories will also help others.

Writing a journal or diary where you can express your experiences or situations when you have suffered emotional pain is difficult, not least because and you might think that, 'I'm not good at writing' or 'I don't want to in case people see it.' or 'I'm worried about what people say' and so on.

Let me reassure that your writing need not be a massive tome (it could be of course) and it is for your eyes only. Others can only see what you have written with your permission. Of course if you feel that you can share your story then please feel free to send it to me[35] and I will share the material in one of my blogs and use your name if you permit this or anonymise to retain your confidentiality.

Remember: Sharing is caring and helps healing

You can start by writing some words about how you feel. For example, low, stressed, dark and pain. You might also want to ask yourself questions, such as:

How do I feel?

Why do I feel this way?

What was my darkest moment?

What moments are the worst when I want to cry? How do I feel at those moments?

Why does my pain not go away?

What can I do?

When will my pain go away?

Can I learn to do something different e.g., use coping techniques?

Try to write in as much detail as possible. You might want to use a diary and answer one or two of these questions every day. You can then look back and see how you have or are coping. There is no doubt that writing about your pain is difficult (and might feel impossible). If you have decided to start writing you will no doubt have some sense of how I feel about writing this book. I know there may be criticism and I hope there will be feedback, but I sincerely hope that it is constructive. I wrote this book as I felt it so important to share my experience.

Try writing. Just start. You will feel better even though your tears may leak out of your eyes and fall down your cheeks. Even crying will release your pain.

Do something creative or something you enjoy as a distraction

Whatever you choose to do it will help distract you from your emotional pain. An activity is a distraction. It is not to help you avoid or ignore your pain. It can be any activity that you enjoy or perhaps one you have not done before. You might decide to take up photography, painting, dancing, or play a musical

---

[35] pat@mindcircles.co.uk – feel free to share your stories of loss, emotional pain or stress. Sharing helps healing.

instrument. You might find that you not only enjoy this activity but that you are very good at it. I tried photography but realised that I could not really match the skills of my son Bruce. I tried painting and discovered that I not only enjoyed it but that I was quite good at it and having shared some of my artwork on social media I received positive comments. Such distraction activities can help you release your emotions which can help in the healing process.

There will be times when you are overwhelmed by your emotional pain and at these times you may find it difficult to manage it. At such times even the act of doing something you enjoy might be too much. Instead, you should do something more simple and easy such as watching a film (preferably not something too sad or intense) or just have a cuppa with a friend, preferably someone who is relaxing to be with and will not cause you pain with questions about how you feel. You just want to sit and enjoy the moment, a time when you do not need to think about your pain. These moments can help you recover your ability to stay calm and control your feelings.

Relaxation techniques

There are many relaxation techniques which can help when you are experiencing emotional pain. After much research, even before I lost Bruce, I realised that most people wanted something simple and easy to use. Therefore, I make no apology for repeating that my ABC techniques (Appendix V) are just that: easy to use, but psychologically proven to work in times of stress and emotional pain. The rationale behind developing my ABC (Appendix V) was that when used and practised regularly, it enables you to change the way you think and act. The technique slows you down and brings you into the present moment to give yourself time to be calm and relaxed.

My 'B' for breathing (Appendix V) is particularly helpful in times of anxiety and stress as it is quick but very effective. One example of this was during an intense court trial[36] when the prosecutor was getting extremely angry and the judge, Lance A. Ito, told her to stop and take three deep breaths. This had the desired effect, reducing, even stopping the anger and making her calm ready to proceed in a professional manner. She also apologised to the judge for her anger.

Of course, in addition to exercising the mind it is important to do physical exercises. Physical exercises can help negative emotions to move and change into more positive emotions. You do not need to undertake vigorous exercise at the gym, although many of you may do this. One of my clients who only worked out his body at the gym without giving his mind a work out became aggressive. When I pointed this out to him, he started doing my ABC techniques and became much more balanced and less aggressive. Indeed, I have found that good trainers at a gym will advise clients on doing both physical and mental exercises. However, as I said you do not need to work out at the gym; you can take a walk in nature as according to psychology research by Berman et al (2008)[37] interacting with nature has

---

[36]   OJ Simpson Murder Trial (1994-1995) – *People of the State of California v Orenthal James Simpson – words of Judge Lance A. Ito – Take 3 deep breaths* – reported in New York Times 24 February 1995 p16.

[37]   Berman, Marc G., Jonides, John and Kaplan, Stephen (2008) *The Cognitive Benefits of Interacting with Nature* Journal of Psychological Science, Vol. 19, Issue 12, pp 1207-1212

cognitive benefits and research by Chowdry (2019)[38] found that connecting with nature helps improve your mental, physical, psychological and emotional wellbeing.

Keep moving forward positively

I focus on moving forward positively for the future. I know Bruce would not want it any other way. That does not mean that I do not have 'down' moments or days. During such moments and days I look for something to distract me.

For the healing process to be effective it is necessary to move forward. You do not want to get trapped in negative feelings too long.

This is where my 'weight' of emptiness plays a part. During the initial shock of any tragic event the 'weight' of your feelings will weigh you down, almost to the brink of drowning. As time goes by if you use the positive techniques then you will find that this 'weight' lightens. Your emotions will not weigh as heavily on you. There will still be moments (maybe days) where the weight is heavy—sometimes too heavy to bear—but if you practise my positive techniques then you will find yourself focusing on a more positive future.

I am not too keen on talking about goals here because sometimes goals are not realistic and may not even be attainable. Instead, focus on making plans. When you make plans to do something that you enjoy and can work towards then it helps the healing process. Making a plan gives you a challenge and helps you to think about the future. This can and will lessen the 'weight of emptiness'.

Power of positive thinking

You may underestimate the power of the mind, but the mind is extremely powerful and when you think positively it can help you to change your mood and the way you think. If you have experienced a tragic event, then positive thinking helps to find something good and even meaningful in the situation. You can think about what you learned from the experience or how you can turn this tragic event into an opportunity to change positively for the future.

> *Remember: from your greatest challenges comes your greatest strength*

From my experience and from stories shared by you, I know that you have found strength that you did not even know you had when faced by tragic, horrendous events.

Of course, you need to find something that will work for you and more than that, you need to stick to it. Time does not take away your feelings, but you can heal. Be brave and resilient: never give up.

> *The weight of emptiness will lessen and you will learn to endure each day more positively.*

---

[38]   Chowdry, Madhuleena Roy (2019) *The Positive Effects of Nature on Your Mental Well-Being* Positive Psychology, 13, October 2019

Getting support

If you are finding it difficult to cope using some of these exercises, then it is important to acknowledge that and seek out professional medical help. In addition to this there are support groups that you can turn to as social and emotional outlets. As I referred to earlier, my writing exercise helps in the healing process but talking helps too. When you talk out loud to someone else about your feelings, this act can help the healing process. However be careful that you do not fall into the trap of repeatedly talking about your situation and emotions as this can be unhealthy and you will get trapped in a negative cycle. You may have someone close that you can talk to—a friend or family member—but regardless whether it is a close friend or support group it is important that you feel safe and secure when talking to them.

From personal experience I did not feel the need or wish to speak with a counsellor probably because I lectured in psychology and was tutor to many students who wanted to become counsellors. In business networking I also came across many coaches and NLP (neuro-linguistic practitioners) and CBT (cognitive behavioural therapists). Among all of these counsellors and coaches there were many of them in my view that I would not want to speak with as in my opinion they did not have the necessary empathetic qualities that I would have wanted. I should not generalise as I know there are some excellent counsellors and coaches around who do amazing work in helping people through the healing process.

However, this route was not for me as I am fortunate to have some wonderful friends and colleagues who gave me what I needed and that was 'space'. They would just be there to sit and listen. As I have said before I am also fortunate that I am able to talk! I talked and still do talk about Bruce. I even talk to him! This gives me comfort and hope.

My experience of attending a support group

I do want to say that I went to a support group with a friend whose child had been murdered. My heart went out to her as she had not only to suffer the loss of her child but also to go through the process of waiting for the matter to go to trial. I remember the day as if it were yesterday. It was only one month after Bruce had committed suicide. We met in a local pub and openly talked about our experience.

I told how I felt about her loss (as it seemed so much more to bear then me) but as mentioned earlier she said that each person experiences loss and the pain of loss in their own way. We also found things to laugh about and at one point we remarked that people around us would never have guessed that we had lost a loved child!

My friend then said she had to leave early as she was going to a meeting. When I asked what the meeting was about, she told me that it was a support group for parents who have lost a child. I asked if I could go with her and she said it was open to anyone who had lost a child.

I attended the support group that night. I felt privileged to listen to the stories shared by those around the table about the loss of their child, but I felt great sadness and distress at the emotional pain they were still experiencing over tragic circumstances, which for some, had taken place many years ago.

One lady shared that this group was the only outlet when she could speak of her son as on the day he died (some 15 years before) her husband had told her that the son's name was never to be mentioned again. In my mind I was thinking if that had been me I would have told my husband to leave!

Others shared stories which were equally if not more heart-breaking. One lady shared that she had lost her daughter just after her 18th birthday. She had been given driving lessons and passed her test just after her birthday. She proudly set off in the car for her first drive but horrifically a huge lorry hit the car and she was killed. Again, this accident had taken place many years before.

My heart went out to all those who shared their stories but I found it even more heart-breaking that (to me) many had not moved forward and were stuck in the negative path of excruciating emotional pain.

I decided that such support groups were not for me. I have also noticed that some groups on social media seem to be an outlet for sharing only the negative. I use social media for personal and business reasons and I do try to find something constructive and positive to say even in the most tragic circumstances. I urge you to try to do the same. Sharing helps you heal but it is most effective if the focus is on moving forward positively.

Over the years I have suffered heartbreak, nursed the dying and lost loved ones, but the loss of my son, Bruce was the most painful. I have cried in my car, cried in the supermarket, cried in the street. Eventually I had to acknowledge my pain and move towards a more positive way of healing. To do this I regularly practise my ABC techniques for wellbeing.

Emotional pain affects your physical health

Emotional pain is just as serious as physical pain although they are not often regarded as equals in society. However, any emotional or mental health issues impact on your physical health and overall wellbeing. When you suffer a loss, you will feel sad: this is a natural emotion. However, if you continue to have feelings of sadness, they can lead to depression which can and should be treated by professionals.

The reality about losing a loved one is that you will grieve forever but you will, with my techniques, and if required, professional support learn to live with your loss. You will endure each day learning to rebuild yourself around your loss. You will never be the same. However if you find yourself experiencing only feelings of sadness for consecutive days without having any positive feelings or thoughts then you should consult a medical professional as feeling this way, even for a few days, will affect your daily life. You should also be open about whether you have turned to alcohol or other substances to deal with your feelings.

Other basic emotions related to loss or trauma are anger, worry, anxiety, fear, even feelings of shame and guilt. These feelings incite the release of adrenaline which increases muscle tension and leads to shallow breathing rather than deep, effective breathing. This is what is known as the fight/flight/freeze response which happens when faced with harmful events, attacks or threats to your survival. The response enables you to move away from danger. However, if you do not cope with emotions such as anger, worry, anxiety, fear, shame and guilt they can lead to long-term physical ill-health.

If you experience any of the above feelings and the techniques you are using are not helping you to cope, you should seek advice from the appropriate medical professionals.

What you are seeking should be overall psychological wellbeing. This is a combination of feeling good and functioning effectively. There is much psychological research on wellbeing and researchers have found that if you have no distress, this does not necessarily imply that you have a high level of psychological wellbeing. Having a high level of psychological wellbeing does not mean feeling happy and doing well, but feeling capable, well-supported and satisfied with your life. Research indicates that if you have a high level of psychological wellbeing then you are more likely to live a long and healthy life.

If you enjoy positive psychological wellbeing then you are likely to have your basic needs met, live in a safe area with sufficient food and adequate shelter.

You can improve your psychological wellbeing and will feel better by carrying out the techniques described above.

In addition to these techniques you should try to:

- have a purpose such as being kind, helping and encouraging others. Start by thinking about how you want to be remembered. Make some notes on what you will do to achieve this. What makes you get up every day (more than just money, although we need money to live).
- carry out acts of kindness. This reminds you that you do have the power to make a difference. When you do this, you will also feel happier and think more positively. Be grateful as this helps you focus on the good things in your life. This may sound simple but if you do it every day it does improve your psychological wellbeing.
- to feel confident and capable and you can do this by reminding yourself of your strengths. Ask yourself what you are good at or what positive traits you have. Or, ask yourself what you have achieved and what qualities you must achieve success.
- let go of past hurt and anger. When you forgive, this does not mean forgetting or letting someone hurt you. Letting go lets you move on in a positive way. As I referred to earlier, Bruce found this very difficult. He just could not let go of his anger against his father. No matter how many times I told him to let go and that the best form of revenge was to be happy and succeed, he could not do it.
- form a deep connection with someone else. There is a difference between being lonely and being alone. Bruce, like me, loved to be alone to think and create. However, if being alone means that you are lonely then that is not good for your emotional and physical health. Simply being around other people is not the solution either. It is important to form a close connection with others. It might just be one or two people, but it is about quality and not quantity. You must also remember that social media is not a substitute for having face-to-face connections with people.

If you regularly practice all the above techniques, you will see how these impact on your positivity and overall mental and physical health.

My main goal in life is to have inner success and inner happiness as I describe in *7 Attributes for Success and Happiness*[39]. I know many of you will pursue lots of goals—some may be unrealistic but that is fine if you do not get anxious about not achieving them all. Some of you may work hard to make money because you believe that this will make you happy. However, if you concentrate solely on making money, then this alone will not make you happy. If you focus on the job or work that brings you in money then you are likely to feel happy. That is often why entrepreneurs are happy because they are doing something they love while they make money (or hope they do!).

Other goals you may have can include having the perfect relationship, perfect body or everyone's approval or all of these and more. These may make you happy but often you become anxious and stressed when you do not achieve these goals. Even when you achieve these goals you may not be genuinely happy. So, how do you achieve this inner happiness? You can work on having inner happiness if you work on having positive thoughts. Remember that the mind is extremely powerful and you can change your thoughts to be more positive.

You can start by looking at your lifestyle and then your attitude about life and what happens to you each day. You probably already know that optimists tend to be happier but this is not because they put on a happy face or always look on the bright side of life. They have certain traits or characteristics. Happy people often tend to believe that they are the masters of their own fate and not victims of circumstances. Try to see the challenges of life like opportunities rather than threats. When you frame it this way you will come up with more effective solutions to the challenges and also feel more elated about dealing with such circumstances.

I know there is much talk about work–life balance but to achieve inner happiness you should try to have a balanced lifestyle. This means including time for:

- connecting socially with friends and family
- personal development
- physical and mental health exercises
- career and work for financial security.

All areas of your life are important so when looking at how you want to achieve a balanced lifestyle you might want to draw a chart, dividing it into equal parts representing the above areas.

Once you have drawn a chart, look at each area and consider whether you give that area what I call SA or FA. When I give my talks I know the FA causes laughter but I do not mean F as in f*@$!!

I mean SA as in some attention and FA as in full attention.

What does that mean I hear you say. Here is a quick exercise.

---

[39]   Elliot, Patricia (2010) *7 Attributes for Success and Happiness* Authorhouse available on www.mindcircles.co.uk and www.stepsforsuccess.co.uk

Think about the last time you went shopping. Did you fully concentrate on what you were buying or was your mind racing, full of other questions such as who will pick the kids up from school, do they have a party to go to, what will we have for tea, did I forget an appointment etc. etc.

If you are honest with yourself, there's a good chance that your mind usually races and is full of other matters. This is what I call having some attention (SA) on what you are doing.

What I ask you to do is fully focus on the activity you are doing—this means you will give full attention (FA) to that activity. It is a difficult exercise but it helps bring balance.

Remember you need to learn how to say NO to taking on too many activities in your life. If you have a partner or children you are probably already committed to many activities that are not your own activities!

At the beginning of a new year you have probably made New Year's Resolutions (goals). Take a moment to think about these resolutions. Did you keep them? Perhaps one or two but not others. The reason usually is, as I have referred to above, that you have set unrealistic goals. That aside, if you failed to achieve one of your goals, how did you feel? Did you just give up, telling yourself that you are a failure? Did you experience feelings of defeat? Maybe?

You should not give up on your goals or resolutions. You should reflect on whether they were unrealistic or whether you thought you could make positive changes in your life overnight.

So, what steps should you take?

- Set realistic, achievable goals—small steps at a time.
- Praise yourself for any progress you make.
- Talk to positive, supportive people and tell them about your goals and successes.

If you follow these steps you are more likely to succeed and not give up. You will feel more confident to follow through on all your goals.

Writing about these techniques and what steps you should take to create a more balanced, happier lifestyle is emotional for me. Bruce was the one person who provided me with some of the techniques and supported me in everything I did.

> *I say again...............If only...................Bruce could have practised what he preached!*

In addition to these techniques I have developed MindBites meditations:

- to help you cope in challenging times
- to help your healing process
- to help you move forward more positively towards overall improved wellbeing.

I continue to write blogs and create podcasts on bereavement and loss as well as other life issues. Please feel free to contact me if you have a particular topic that you wish me to address.

I sincerely hope that my sharing of my experience of losing Bruce, and the other stories shared by those who have lost a loved one will help you to realise that you are not alone. Each person will experience loss in different ways but what brings us all together is knowing we are not alone. There are coping techniques (Appendix V) which can help the healing process and if used regularly will help you move forward yet still leave you with memories of your loved one.

Life is awesome, forget the what if...or the if only...

Are you always looking for something else or someone else (the grass is greener approach)?

If the answer is yes, then you think you are focusing on the future but you are actually focusing on what you do not have.

This can be especially true about money. I often hear people say something like, 'if only I had more money or if only I won the lottery....' Now, I am not saying that would not be nice and you do need money to live but do not just focus on money.

Be grateful

Take a moment to think about what you have now. I know this can be difficult particularly if you have suffered loss and trauma but there are things in life that you have no control over. You can only improve your 'self' when you learn to accept who you are, and this can be very challenging.

You can realise your true potential by being spontaneous and by embracing the unexpected.

All around you are bombarded with information, telling you to focus on what you want, who you want to be and so on. What this is really doing is telling you that you must change and what you have just now is not enough. This is fine, to an extent. However, I know some people may not be happy with whatever they get or have. Therefore, what I am asking you to think about is to be aware of what you have now (in the present); be grateful. Make a gratitude list. Sometimes the greatest gift arrives when you least expect it, even when you do not want or need it.

Remember some of the greatest events or connections you make in life do not come about because you have been working hard to get them but come about unexpectedly.

Life is awesome and it will continue to surprise you if you let it. Do not always think about 'what if' or 'if only'.

As my book is ready for publication, I look back on what I had to do. I had to think about the words I would write which was very challenging (as I seek perfection)! I also knew that there were some things that were said that might have been hurtful but my intent has never been to hurt anyone. My aim is to raise awareness of what can lead to mental health issues no matter the circumstances.

Most challenging and emotional of all was going through Bruce's notebooks, artwork books and photographs. I felt as if I was invading his privacy; something he valued highly.

Tears are flowing as I write these last few words: I had to look back on the part I played in his life. This was extremely difficult as I found myself constantly thinking I could have been a better parent; I could have done more. The constant 'what if' or 'if only' were almost too much to bear. I then had to stop myself and use my own MindBites[40] meditations to help me cope and understand that as a mother I did the best I could with the tools I had at the time. There is no university to learn how to become a parent although I can hear Bruce's words now: 'there should be!'

I hope that this book will help others who have had or are still experiencing a life similar to mine but more specifically I sincerely hope it brings comfort and hope to those who have lost a loved one and those who are struggling with depression, anxiety and thoughts of suicide.

For my gorgeous son Bruce— your life was awesome but you did not realise it, thinking about the 'what if' or the 'if only'; always striving for perfection; being too hard on yourself. I love you always RIP.

> *'I can see clearly now the rain has gone, all of the bad feelings have disappeared*
> *Gone are the dark clouds that had me blind, I think I can make it now the pain is gone*
> *Here's the rainbow I've been praying for, look all around there's nothing but blue skies*
> *It's gonna be a bright, bright sunshiny day'*

---

[40]   MindBites meditations www.mindcircles.co.uk and www.stepsforsuccess.co.uk

BRUCE'S LAST LETTER TO ME

Dated 3rd May 2014 and time 13.51.

'Dearest Mummy

It's truly no-one's fault. I just wasn't a well bunny. There was <u>NO FOUL PLAY!</u>

I've done the washing, cleaned up, weird kinda feels normal, just doing stuff, but anyways' Mummy, it's no-bodies fault really. I dunno, it's just that I was trapped in another character, ...I love my brother (R) dearly, so dearly and my sister (G) so so much and my see sis (K) so so much too! Please keep my notebooks/artbooks for reference too.

Look on the bright side, Dad can read my obituary – there the connection might be made at last!!

But to you my dear I'm sorry so so sorry. But it's gonna rock where I'm going, Rock.

Much love as always. Bruce xx

P.S. you'll need John's number I can't work obviously......

Mummy, He's the best! TELL HIM all the best with family and all.

P.P.S. Darling, there's some cash for you. I owe nothing to anybody!

JANE PATMORE—CELEBRANT'S TRIBUTE TO BRUCE

'What is it to die but to stand naked in the wind and to melt into the sun?
And what is it to cease breathing but to free the breath from its restless tides,
That it may rise and expand and be unencumbered?'

Gathering and Welcome

You can shed tears that he is gone
Or you can smile because he lived,
You can close your eyes and pray that he will come back
Or you can open your eyes and see all that he has left,
Your heart can be empty because you can't see him
Or you can remember him, and only that he is done
Or you can cherish his memory and let it live on.

Thank you all for coming.

We are here this afternoon to pay our respects, and to honour the life of Bruce, to remember him with love and affection, and to offer our support for his closest family and friends.

Death, in a way unites us all, and Bruce's death means that for a time today, each one of us has put aside our work, our worries, the busyness of our lives, to join together with everyone here, sharing in a common bond of love for Bruce and a common bond of sadness at his passing.

I hope that at the end of this service for Bruce you will take comfort from knowing that you took the opportunity to remember him and honour him, and to grieve in the company of family and friends who also knew and loved him. This is a time to express the whole range of feelings that arise at a time like this. So whether you knew him as Bruce, Brucy-boy, your son, your brother, your uncle, your neighbour or your friend, be glad that you had him in your life, and that you brought love and belonging onto his. The writer C.S. Lewis said: 'when pain or loss is to be borne, a little courage helps more than much knowledge, a little human sympathy helps more than much courage, and the tincture of love helps more than all'. And so, on behalf of Bruce's family, I'd like to thank you for your human sympathy and your love. It means a great deal to them that you have come to join them to recall the years of Bruce's life. Your presence here is important, for it is friends who stand by you during a turbulent time that are a source of strength and consolation.

Every life, including our own, is precious. We have each had our experiences of life and death, with different memories and different feelings of love, grief and respect. Today is an opportunity to express our beliefs and our feelings and to acknowledge our loss and our sadness. All who mourn need support and consolation. Our presence here is part of that support for each other and particularly for Bruce's family.

The former poet laureate, Andrew Motion, wrote that funerals establish connections between us, as well as marking a separation. They bring families and friends together, and they link the living to the departed. Part of our service today will bring Bruce close to our thoughts with vivid memories, yet this is also a time for stepping away, and letting go. Today we might be moved to tears, and we might also look for perspective—understanding that we cope with loss not by forgetting Bruce, but by finding out how we can best live with our memories of him. And so, I invite you now to quietly turn your thoughts to Bruce, and to his family, and to whatever beliefs you hold in your heart. Please join me in a moment of quiet thought:

> *In the spirit of love and remembrance, we gather here, honouring our memories of Bruce, allowing ourselves even in the midst of grief to remember him with gladness in our hearts. May the memories of precious moments shared with Bruce support us at this time and be a source of strength rather than sadness. We feel thankful for the years that Bruce lived and for all the good things that were shared with him. Our hearts feel sad at the moment, but we know that this feeling will soften as time passes. Though we meet here in mourning today, we are supported by compassion of others, and we trust that the love of good friends and family will never fail us. May our individual beliefs and our shared humanity sustain us as we bring our grief, seeking comfort for today and courage for tomorrow (Amen).*

Hymn

At a time like this we seek comfort and consolation in many ways—physical, emotional, spiritual; we look for solace in nature or words or music. Often, we find something reassuring in familiarity. So, I invite you to stand and join in singing *The Lord's My Shepherd*....

Tributes

Bruce was born on 4th March, eldest son of N and Patricia, and elder brother to a brother and two sisters. However, our service here this afternoon is not about the facts and the chronology of Bruce's life, it's about the characteristics and the talents that made Bruce the unique individual that each of you knew.

Bruce grew up in Glasgow, living firstly in a small village, then in a suburb of Glasgow and later in the west end. His brother and sisters describe this time as a rather free-spirited, bohemian lifestyle when they ran around with a big gang of friends, exploring their world and getting into mischief: turning the drawing room into a snooker room, setting up a rope swing in the stairway so they could swing out of the open front door, or mixing up a bucket of all the ingredients from the kitchen which they could tip from the first floor window onto the heads of unsuspecting friends who came to play. Being close in age, and learning about life and growing up together, Bruce and his brother had a strong relationship. For many years they shared a room; with his brother's half decorated with pictures of Sam Fox and Playboy bedclothes, while Bruce's half had colours and stripes in the style of Mondrian. Sharing a room must have been difficult for someone who valued his privacy as much as Bruce, and so one day his brother came home to find that Bruce had erected a curtain down the middle of the room to keep his side unseen.

And in case you are imagining some kind of harmonious childhood idyll, the closeness in age and the strong competitive streak in both boys meant that Bruce and his brother also fought—a lot. In fact Bruce's brother says that most of his injuries resulted from times when he and Bruce were fighting: the scars on his legs and arms, or the finger nearly chopped off when they were fighting over who sat in the driving seat of their Dad's minivan which their mother drove. So who would have thought that it was a good idea for either Bruce or his brother to have a set of Japanese throwing knives bought from the Barras? And who would have thought that it was a good idea for four children to take to Sunday School all the best and newest tricks from a joke shop? And yes, after setting off one too many stink bombs, they were effectively expelled with the Sunday School teacher suggesting to their Mum, that it might be better not to bring them back.

Over recent days, the family have been remembering holidays to Achiltibuie, or Spain, with their Dad always sporting the latest camcorder, each one with a larger and heavier pack to be carried. But some things are never recorded by an adult. Bruce and his brother making a den in their grandparents' attic and secretly drinking the hidden stash of Appletiser, or working out how to get the key to the pantry and raid the supply of their Dad's favourite orange Club biscuits, or the Christmas when they sent the youngest family member, their sister into her parents room, taking the mumbled replies as agreement that they could open their presents. Imagine that chaos: four children, a pile of unwrapped presents, and no idea of who had given what.

In the midst of all of this, Bruce's traits and character could be seen. He was the only one in the family who could complete a Rubik's cube—without peeling the stickers off or taking it apart with a screwdriver—and he starred as Tweedledum in Alice Through the Looking Glass. He mastered the art of dramatic timing and delivery, so even before the film Trainspotting was released, Bruce had obtained a copy of the screen play and had everyone in stitches as he recited passages from it.

Bruce was creative and artistic, a great reader who was hugely intelligent and loved a debate. He had phenomenal ideas and his brain was always full of things. Bruce had a great memory, he could recite poems and quote from books and he would recall the details of life: a pair of shoes, or a conversation that others had long forgotten. Yet he was also meticulous about recording information, cataloguing all his photos and writing everything down in his notebooks. He wanted others to understand what he understood, and love what he had loved, suggesting films they might like, or books they should read.

Bruce's creativity meant that he could visualise art and opportunity where others only saw rubbish, and many of you have been called to help him salvage a door from a skip, or rescue old computers from an office, been chastised for throwing away an unused curtain rail, or asked to store the pedestal for a sink in your house. Yet to see some of these works finished, such as an old bookcase, revamped, restored, recreated into something new, was to appreciate the vision and talent that Bruce had.

Yet alongside his creativity and intelligence, aspects of Bruce's character could make life difficult for him. He was a non-conformist: original but sometimes not quite fitting in; a perfectionist but feeling let down by his own imperfections; spontaneous but sometimes volatile; appreciative of art but lacking belief in his own talents.

Living in London for a while, Bruce retained his dream of being an actor. He could connect with people from all walks of life and made a big impact amongst the people he met. Bruce's PR photos from that time detail all the stage plays and films in which he had lead roles and supporting roles, the commercials in which he took part, and his special skills: accents, (including Upscale English, Cockney, and Scottish dialects); stage combat and juggling. Then when Bruce went to Hollywood to take a role in a film, in typically paradoxical manner, he realises that he would rather be behind the camera than in front of it. He completed a diploma in photography but more than the learning he was inspired by his mentor, the journalistic photographer Martin Gilfeather, who gave him a camera, lent him specialist lenses and ignited his passion for photography.

Bruce worried about the impact of trusting people, and at times walked a difficult tightrope, not always able to get the balance right. He wanted to be open, to share, and yet was worried after he had done so in case he had shown too much of himself. He would drive forward on business projects with his brother, then back off suddenly when the possibility of success became overwhelming. He sought recognition for his talent and art, yet desperately wanted to remain hidden. Nothing offers a better example of this than Bruce's website. Created to publish his photography, a domain name was registered and the website was set up. Initially it didn't meet Bruce's requirements: he wanted it black. And so a black background was created. But no, that's not what Bruce had in mind. What he wanted was a website that was completely black, something that didn't show his work at all, but something that made people interested enough and caused them to think and wonder, and then perhaps to see his photos.

There is so much you remember about Bruce, and it is not possible to do justice to it all this afternoon. He was a good swimmer and was in the school swimming team; he loved cricket and Manchester United; he looked after himself, could be fanatical about nutrition, and pushed himself physically—cycling, or showing his flexibility one year at Christmas time, by demonstrating the Lotus position, and then encouraging others to try the same.

Bruce had a marked sense of style, so he could match Primark jeans with a designer scarf, round it off with a five euro watch, and still look wonderful.

Bruce was very practical and willing: he worked hard and enthusiastically helping his young sister with the refit of her Dad's kitchen or updating the bathroom at his Mum's house. And yet in many of these projects there remains just one little thing that is not quite complete—the piece of mosaic tile in the kitchen that doesn't quite stick, or the last couple of tiles in his Mum's bathroom.

Bruce was a fantastic uncle to his seven nieces and nephews. He loved them all. He made no allowance for their young ages if he was competing against them. And they loved him and enjoyed his company in the special way that children do with a favourite uncle who has no children of his own, and therefore always seems more willing to play. In fact recently one of his nieces asked her Mum: 'Is Uncle Bruce an adult?'

So, Bruce was childlike, a gentle soul, artistic, creative, yet tormented by his own perfectionism, and lack of self-belief. Nothing that other people could say to him could take away how he felt about himself, and despite considerable talents, and the love and support that was given to him, Bruce took his own life. At such a time, there are moments when we recall the difficult times in someone's life and wonder if we did enough: for this is part of our grief in all deaths. However, beyond these difficult times for Bruce, there were many years, and periods when all of you here, in your own ways, and at different times, offered to Bruce the love, the support, the acknowledgement, companionship, stimulation and hope that made his life worth living for so long. There are so many people whose lives have been touched: people from London, from across Scotland, from Glasgow, from further afield; New York, LA, Barcelona, Cuba.

It is difficult to find words that express in any adequate way, the mixture of love and sadness that are felt. But Bruce's brother has chosen some beautiful words written by Bruce's friends over the last days as they dealt with their own shock and recalled favourite times and incidents with Bruce.

(Bruce's brother reads memories of his brother and tributes written by others).

(Bruce's sister (G) reads her tribute and although his wee sis (K) did not read a tribute I know her heart was breaking.)

(My tribute (See Appendix III))

The Committal

We have heard some thoughts of Bruce, but you all remember him in your own special way. As we prepare to say goodbye to Bruce's physical presence, I invite you as you sit, to offer thanks for every memory that you hold: for Bruce and what he meant to each of you; for the sadness that you feel at the sudden loss of him from your life and yet also for the many days when you shared time together, laughed or played together, spoke with one another, fought one another, or walked alongside each other in gentle companionship.

We are not meant to avoid life in fear of death. We are meant to live each moment fully, to connect with our environment and the people in our lives, to share the best of ourselves generously, to have courage to do what needs to be done, and to practice our own deepest convictions. As we honour Bruce's memory, and come together for support, make us more aware of the peace and comfort that comes from sharing this time with others.

In honour of the life that Bruce lived, I invite you to stand together for the committal.

Tenderly, and with honour and appreciation we remember the life of Bruce.

Bruce is now beyond harm, beyond fear and pain, and wondering:

So here...in this last ritual....in sorrow, but without fear, in love and appreciation, we commit his body to be cremated.

We trust Bruce's spirit unto all the mysteries of love and mercy. Earth to earth, ashes to ashes, dust to dust.

Bruce, we honour your life we accept your departure, and we cherish your memory.

Time for reflection

We will now take a few moments to hold Bruce in our hearts and reflect upon how he touched our lives personally as we listen to the wonderful music of Hallelujah sung by Jeff Buckley.

Closing words

It is said that neither death nor life, neither angels nor demons, neither the present nor the future, nor any powers, neither height nor depth, nor anything else in all creation, will be able to separate us from the love that surrounds us, and remains in our hearts.

As you talk about Bruce in the days and years to come, you will reminisce and laugh and cry. Today is his physical presence that we are leaving, not his personality, character and spirit which will live on forever in your thoughts and memories.

Immediately after this service the family will be leaving, but they thank you all for coming, and extend a very warm invitation to you all to join them this afternoon at a rugby club, part of a local sports club where you'll have an opportunity to greet the family, share your own memories of Bruce's life, and also to see some examples of his awe inspiring photography. There is also here a collage of photos of Bruce. As you leave, take time to stop and look, and remember, enjoying his youthful looks and his sense of style. And for those who can't make it to the rugby club this afternoon, there is a book, which you are invited to sign.

When a loved one dies there are many ways to remember them, and I close with a few lines written by Khalil Gibran in his book The Prophet:

> *For life and death are one, even as the river and the sea are one.*
> *For what is it to die but stand naked in the wind and to melt into the sun?*
> *And what is it to cease breathing but to free the breath from its restless tides, that it*
> *may rise and expand and be unencumbered?*
> *Only when you sip from the river of silence shall you indeed sing.*
> *And when you have reached the mountain top, then you shall begin to climb.*
> *And when the earth shall claim your limbs, then shall you truly dance.*

As we leave, we will hear the music of Johnny Nash singing, 'I can see clearly now....' This is a sad day, and it is also a day when we cling to the hope of moments when the pain has lessened, some of the bad feelings have disappeared, we see the rainbow we've been searching for and we trust that one day it's gonna be a bright (bright), bright (bright) sun-shiny day... Thank you for being here today.

MY TRIBUTE TO MY GORGEOUS SON BRUCE

Thank you, Jane, for capturing Bruce to a 'T'.

Bruce you are my gorgeous talented son. You are my first born. I love you so much. When you came into my life I saw the sun. You had that soulful look in your eyes and I had this feeling that you had been here before.

You always questioned everything. I was often called to the school because you had been put out of the class—I would ask why and be told that you had kept asking questions. You never understood why that was a problem (neither did I). You desperately wanted answers for everything and when they were not given to you, you tried to find them; always searching, forever searching. Your breadth and depth of reading goes beyond anyone else I know: politics, art, psychology and much, much more. You brought me academic articles on many subjects that I should include in my work. I just hope you are not causing too much trouble in heaven with your questioning!

You were always creative; writing, drawing and making things out of anything— a sculptor, actor, poet, writer, photographer— an eclectic artist. In the words of D.W. Winnicott:

'You are the artist in which there is an inherent dilemma – the dark and the light, the urgent need to communicate yet the still more urgent need not to be found'

Your first love was swimming, then snowboarding, skiing, football (Partick Thistle, Man. United – our recent chat about Liverpool – I'm sure you'll be influencing who wins from up there), you played 5-a-side in the park…but I have chosen some words from the many written by you in your artwork and reference books— it's about cricket— I think it sums you up – the dark and the light.

Crickety Boo (by Bruce)

Cricket is a theatre, it's dance; it's an opera; it's dramatic; it's about individual conflict that takes place on a huge stage but the two warriors also represent the ten other players; it's a relationship between the one and the many. The individual and the social, the leader and the follower, the individual and the universal.

I am overwhelmed by the messages of support from round the globe… Too many to read them all but here are some from your secondary school mates. His smile could melt hearts; from friends near and far—charismatic, inspirational; loved by all; touched everyone's mind and heart; from a close friend—for every moment of sadness I'm strangely overwhelmed with huge smiles and belly laughter remembering his hugely fun character; Bruce is a massive part of all our lives in London; incredibly creative, without fear, always chasing an adventure; a super enthusiastically infectious, handsome, charismatic, charming, eloquently spoken and always dapperly dressed young Scottish spoken man! I was definitely envious of his suave and charismatic smooth skills not just with the ladies but everyone he came to be in the company of; and much, much more.

I have so much still to say to you, but I know in the months and years to come I will keep speaking to you and I will ensure that your talents will never be forgotten. I will miss our Sundays ('Politics Now') and you were so pleased that I was playing the piano again (the piano – a gift from a good friend).

I know you believe in me. I believed in you so much and wished you had believed in yourself. People from all walks of life around the globe loved you simply for being you—you had no snobbishness or arrogance within you—and you took everyone as you found then. You could meet the Queen in the morning and turn to speak to Jimmy in the street. You could stand tall and hold your own among lords and ladies and yet feel at home with Cuban street domino players. When you travelled afar it was not as a tourist but to be among the local people. You loved your brother and sisters and only recently said to me 'little sis has style' (which you teased she must have got from you!) but you only wished you had even some of her business acumen...You often said you wanted one child and would lavish all your love on that child—his legacy to you all is to say, every day, 'I love you' to your children.

You wrote to me that you felt trapped in another character: you now have the biggest role of your life watching over us all.

I know this is not goodbye—in the poem 'All is Well' by Henry Scott Holland—death is nothing at all... you have only slipped into the next room...I am I and You are You....I will speak to you in the easy way which I always used...you have left your heart with me. Your love is deep within me and it reaches me from the stars...no matter where you are, or I am, I feel your love. We will laugh as we always laughed... because laughter is the sunshine which dissolves the darkness.

As the collage shows:

Bruce – you are darkness, you are light; you are a thousand winds that blow; you are the diamonds in the snow; you are the sunshine in the rain; when I walk the dog you are the swift uplifting rush of wind; you are the birds circling in flight and you are the soft star shining at night.

As a creative adult the child in you survived and that child will survive in all our minds. You were young in looks and in heart and now you will be young forever and as you wrote to me...it's going to rock where you're going.

Everyone is all the more rich in spirit for having known you. You are the once in a lifetime kind of person.

I am honoured to have given birth to you and to have known you. You will always be my boy. Lots of love and hugs. Mummy xx.

SHARING HELPS HEALING - STORIES OF LOSS

Sharing of grief can lighten the 'weight' so here are some wonderful stories and poems. Let those tears flow down your cheeks. Crying is good for your soul, but also remember the beautiful memories of the time you shared together.

The following stories have touched me, and I am deeply honoured to include them in this book. Please note that permission has been given by these wonderful people to me to include their stories here. Where no name is mentioned, these individuals have requested that they remain anonymous. Nonetheless they have shared their stories with heart-felt emotion knowing that they will help others.

There is much reference globally to there being a need for people to 'talk' or ask for help in relation to mental health issues including suicide. This is easier said than done and I have already mentioned the fact that Bruce would talk about mental health, but on a more academic level, disconnected from his own troubles.

In view of this I felt it important to share a story from someone who suffered a breakdown to the extent that she felt suicidal. She is not alone in having such thoughts and feelings.

Sharing thoughts and feelings of depression and suicide

'I had a bit of a breakdown a while ago and was suicidal. At the time I didn't know if I should say anything as I didn't want to upset people or have them think I was being ridiculous. It was a really awful time. I got through it because I didn't want my children thinking I had left them I knew they wouldn't be able to understand. I was just so depressed and isolated. I couldn't see a way out. I knew telling people would make me look weak or attention seeking so there was no point. I'm not ashamed of it I now feel I could get through almost anything on my own as a result. I really tried to get help from doctors and there was literally none. I couldn't admit quite how bad it was in case they thought I was affecting my kids who were very much protected from it. I've never felt so alone. People should know how incredibly hard it is to ask for or get help when you're struggling that much and I don't have the means to speak up and even if I did I'd be vilified.......". Anon

> *It is NOT being weak to admit to having mental health problems or to talk about them or ask for help. Many individuals (like my son Bruce) do not or may not want to admit*

to having mental health problems and certainly do not want to talk about them or ask for help. You also need a trusting environment in which to talk. To do so, so seek professional help when you can. It is also NOT easy for people to reach out either whether it is a family member, friend or colleague.

Loss of a baby

Samantha shares her beautiful poem on the loss of her baby '*......we didn't know the gender but we felt that she was a Sofia...........I could only bring myself to write the poem last year so it's taken a long time to process my emotions and be willing to write them down*'. I am honoured to be able to include this poem and know that many will empathise with her experience and feel her pain as you read it.

They say don't blame yourself but you do,
They say it happens to one in 3, but I just think about you
They say they can't explain the reasons why
But I sit there motionless and I cry

I cry with my whole body, tears seeping through my pores
I cry so much my muscles ache and my body's sore
I go over why it happened again, again and again
Is it something I did, when will this pain end

Life just carries on, but you are left behind
Still heavy on my heart, filling up my mind
I imagine you in my arms, smiling up at me
Instead you're up in heaven, happy and carefree.

I miss you like it was yesterday
I will always miss you forever
That day, I lost you my darling
But one day, we will again be together
Best wishes
Samantha Allen.

Loss of a son

A wonderful sharing by a Mum, Gwyn, on the loss of her son, Jamie.

We lost our son, Jamie, just over two years ago, 18.10.17, 5 days after his 33rd birthday when he took his own life. Our life stood still that day and never re started in the same way. He was son, grandson, brother, uncle and husband and father to three girls he called his diamonds. Their loss has become our focus and helps most days to keep the feelings of being swamped from overwhelming us. Our lives appear in two parts before and after. So many came to his funeral and shared their memories which were a help, not only that day but in all the days since. There is a huge whole left and we muddle along as best we can. We find sharing our experiences helps, not just us but others who have gone through similar loss. It's like assembling a family of people who understand our sense of helplessness, who have the same unanswered questions that we will never know the answers to. He was not a coward but the bravest person I know, who believed he was saving everyone from the pain he was going through. We just wish there was an alternative option for him to have taken, there is some small comfort in knowing for him his pain was ended that day.

I want to add here that when I asked Gwyn if she would allow her son's name to be used – she wrote telling me that her son's name 'is' Jamie. I found the use of the present tense poignant and powerful as he is with her always in her heart and soul, just like my gorgeous boy Bruce is with me. Gwyn Morrison.

Loss of a son

A beautiful, poignant story by a Mum on the loss of her son.

I fell in love with Ben, my first born son the moment I laid eyes on him, he was perfect and tiny and I was his mum and I would protect him with my life.

When I heard on the news or read in the paper of a grieving family mourning the loss of their beloved child, I could not imagine how they could ever take another breath, how could they, they had lost the most precious thing in the world, my heart went out to them and it still does.

One happy sunny day I got the call that no parent ever wants, my beautiful Ben had been killed in a road traffic accident. At the time, my husband and I lived in America and we then had to endure an agonising 9 hour flight back to the UK which was full of holiday makers all laughing and talking about what a great time they'd had, I cried for the whole flight, people stared but I didn't care, I just wanted to scream.

Ben's funeral was packed out with family, friends and colleagues all wanting to say a final goodbye to a lovely young man who had so much to live for, it was so incredibly sad. At the gathering after our last goodbye, we had Ben's favourite music playing, one of the songs by Jack Johnson; 'Better together' a beautiful song, reminds me of Ben so much.

Not a day goes by when I do not think of Ben, some days I'm so sad I cannot speak and other days I laugh at some of the funny things he'd say or do. Every Christmas day he'd dress up as Father Christmas with a black plastic bag filled with cushions stuffed up his top and 'Ho Ho Ho' his way down the street ringing a bell much to the amusement of the streets residents.

He was a terrific hands on father to his son who looks like him and is like him in so many ways, this fills me with so much joy and sadness too. Joy because of their remarkable resemblance and sadness because Ben will never see what a terrific person he is. I'm sad because he has never met his nieces and nephews who often talk about him, my granddaughter's will often say they have been talking to Ben and have seen him driving his car, they write him letters and send him cards 'to heaven'......they'd have loved him so much.

Ben was handsome, kind, clever and thoughtful, he was always thinking of others and was always there for his family and friends. We talk about him often and wish so much that he was still here. He is loved and missed beyond words. He was an avid reader........the book he did not finish; 'Jonathan Strange and Mr Norrell' is the book I now have found the strength to read for myself......and for Ben.

I suppose it is easy to say 'how can we ever take another breath' in my case Ben's legacy was love life, be honest, kind, try your best and be happy.

I'm trying to honour Ben's life by doing just that. LB

Loss of a sister

Heartfelt poem written by Katie on the loss of her sister.

No Show

I thought you'd be here today
I've been here an hour
That man spoke about you
But his words hold no power

I know you left quickly
With no words to say
How I could still reach you
And what happened that day

I don't really care
What the stupid man said
You're not in that room
Not a voice in his head

I just can't believe
You'll never be back
How will my life heal?
With this permanent crack.

I dream things are different
You're here and you care
You tenderly hold me
While I touch your hair

I still don't care
What the psychic man said
He can't speak for you
Cause then you'd be dead

Katie White.©

Loss of a sister

A moving tribute written by Dave on the loss of his sister Elaine

I set this page up just after you passed and felt I needed to do this to let people know what had happened and to pay tribute to such an amazing person. I came to a realisation just now after talking with Mam. Maybe I knew it already but never admitted but I have been using this page to talk about you and to others but have never used it to talk to you. I have seen others do it but never actually felt great talking from my perspective to you. I really don't know if you are here and able to take this in but I have those thoughts a lot and just hope we are right. Anyway, here goes. Probably need to do this no matter how long it took.

Hey Sis. Firstly, I would like to say how proud I am to be your brother and have realised even more how amazing of a person you were here. The memories I have are you are so brilliant but I did block them out for so long as it just plain hurt to know that you were taken away from us in such a hugely tragic way. Actually, words cannot even explain the anger and hurt at the realisation that my only sister is not with me and how much I am missing this huge part of my life. Counsellors could not get this out of me and not even family and friends. Instead, I went on "as normal" with this pain and anger building until I caved. I cannot explain either exactly what happened to me but I do remember waking up in hospital and finally being diagnosed with severe depression. I am only realising now, this was bound to happen as I have lost a part of me and my whole life has changed forever. Suppose the label woke me up but at that stage I didn't really care what they called it I just knew I could not go on like this. I still couldn't connect with what happened. I did talk about you and put together things for others but never really accepted the severity of what had happened.

As time went on and I was put somewhat back on track after this I did remember and feel what you have said about others. You were such a caring person and didn't want us to feel pain and be unhappy. This was inevitable but I do take this with me now. It's something to cling onto at least.

I miss you unbelievably, and we experienced so much of the same things together growing up. When we got that bit older, we would talk about everything and talk about all our plans we had for each of our lives and what made us happy and sad. I told you when something went right and wrong and you were always there. When that went, a part of me disappeared but I continued on like I was okay. I knew people looked at me like I was dealing with it well but it did come back on me and very hard.

What you went through and we went through was war. It changes perception of everything. I tried to be "normal" but unfortunately nobody can be after that. Terror, hurt and even guilt has an aftermath and it stayed with me for a long time after you passed and I am feeling somewhat alive again. When you died, I think like others, I did not have motivation to go on. It's hard for others to understand perfectly but the aftermath of war and loss together with lost hope made me want to say that was that. This was all happening without me fully realising what I was feeling and that was a very hard thing to understand. I understand it now and this is why I need to write this.

I would love you to be here with us now, spending time with Andrew, your nephew, which you never met here. I miss sharing the latest happenings still and miss everything that you were. People always say it about a person who passed but I really know that you were an absolutely amazing person and loved by all of us. That made it so hard to come to terms with this. You were so young and had so much to look forward to and I will never have my only sister back. Suppose I have accepted it. Time does help you accept it better but actually I will never fully accept it. All I can do now is make sure to make the most of life and keep your spirit alive. Andrew will always know you as we will talk and share stories and photos. If it was me who went I would want you to be happy now. I do know that. I knew you too well ☺;) *You would be asking everyone if they were okay as well.*

I still have all your texts. Your last text to me read "Thanks for all your support. Keep saying prayers and we will get through it. Love you loads too. X x x chat tomorrow bro x". You got too sick after this. I sometimes feel you knew that time was the last. I remember holding your hand and you just kept crying. That was different to the other times. That time told me enough was enough. You fought hard sis and all I can really say now is that I am glad that you are no longer in pain as that was the hardest. You will always be my big sis.

I miss you lots xxxxxx

Your lil bro, Dave.

Loss of a brother

Shared emotions and feelings from a sister touched by loss of her brother.

I miss him every day. It has been 18 years since I last spoke to my big brother. One minute he was there and the next he was dead.

He was killed in an awful car crash while traveling home from meeting a friend. The memories of that night and days later surrounding the crash never go away. I can put them away for a while but they surface easily at any time. I actively searched for more details years later to help me understand what happened. I read obituaries and stories of other families who have lost family in car accidents and feel their pain. It's just my new normal now.

He was only 24 and was full of fun and love. I miss him being in my life.

Then I lost my dad 3 years ago, it just broke me.

Grief is the hardest thing I have ever had to deal with and you deal with it for the rest of your life. It is such an all-consuming event that can swallow you whole. Thinking about death has become normal but I still don't understand it. One day I will. Xx

Respecting this sister's wishes Anon.

Loss of a stillborn child

Moving, poignant sharing by Natasha on the loss of her stillborn child Harriet.

Harriet Evans. 03.05.1998 – with never ending love.

The loss of your child is something I felt for a long time that my brain could not accept. It is just not what happens is it? You would never think of your own child dying before you.

The painful milestones of my child's life that live deep within my soul that no one ever mentions for example on what would have been her sixteenth, eighteenth, twenty first birthday? Then I wonder are other people imagining and remembering this day too and yet are too scared to remind me or is my child forgotten? It is a pain no human should feel, and I truly believe that unless someone has lost a child - a part of one's own inner being no one can fully understand this unique pain which lives on forever in your heart. A heart, my heart that is broken in places that I never even knew existed. A heart that would never be the same again.

A loss of a child is not an event but an indescribable journey of survival.

At 13 weeks the joy of finding out I was pregnant turned to concern as I assumed, I was miscarrying. At the scan, it was explained to me that there were two eggs like twins, but one egg had not formed properly and was miscarrying. I was naturally sad but the other was perfectly growing. I did have some bleeding throughout the rest of my pregnancy but it progressed to 40 weeks.

We decided to name our daughter Harriet, even before she was born. We prepared excitedly buying baby items, gently preparing Hannah for the arrival of her baby sister. Imagining what she would look like and how close my two girls would be. I was in love already. Cherishing ever kick and movement I felt. The nursery was all ready and I felt overjoyed with the excitement.

At 41 weeks, I sat blankly, blinking staring at the machine, scanning for the flickering heartbeat and the familiar sound of the washing machine heartbeat. Nothing. Not even registering the doctor's gentle explanation that my baby had died. The horror of the next 24 hours of labour was indescribable. Physically and Mentally.

Me feeling what I thought was a kick and my then husband running up the corridor calling for the midwife excitedly that there had been a mistake as now the baby was moving again. She gently came into the room and held my hand but looked at us with sympathy as she explained – this could not be possible, and she was so so sorry, but our baby had died. I felt acutely embarrassed and crushed that we had both believed that this could not be happening and that somehow our baby had come back to life or there had been some terrible mistake.

Having the pain and trauma of the birth with no reward at the end. The cries of new-born's all around me echoing down the corridors, whilst I held tightly onto my lifeless daughter. Not wanting to let her go for fear of not holding her ever again.

My own milk arriving responding to other babies cries in the hospital. It was a true horror and I was completely lost.

The photos that we took, my only memories that she did exist, fully formed and in my arms. Photos that I could never show with pride or put on display because of her blue appearance with contrasts of red as her skin had dissolved in places for fear of another's reaction. Memories that still haunt me to this day but the only memories of my precious child that I will ever have. I was crushed. Sitting alone in the nursery in disbelief. There was no explanation as to why Harriet had died, at the time it was still very much in the news about the Alder Hey scandal, where body parts had been taken from babies without parents' permission and knowledge. It just seemed too much to bear, I just could not take anything else of what life threw at me so we declined a post-mortem. I would spend a lifetime ahead of not knowing why.

Even popping to the local shop was a nightmare for me as people could see my flat stomach and would call out – congratulations! – did you have a boy or girl? Trying to awkwardly explain whilst keeping composed, and then avoiding eye contact as I could not bear or cope with any reaction of sadness, sympathy, embarrassment, pity or shock,

I remember the day of the funeral as if it was yesterday but at the time I remember feeling as if I was watching someone else and it wasn't really me there. The sun was shining, the birds were singing, the trees were blooming with beautiful pink blossom. I even read a poem at the graveside with great composure, sailing through the words unable to look at anyone else. Until it came to the last line of footprints in the sand. "It was then that I carried you" I felt relief I had got to the end of the poem and then my voice cracked and I could see myself tumbling into the freshly dug grave on top of the tiny white coffin. Of course, that never happened. I didn't tumble at all. I just wanted to – I was not ready to let go of my beloved daughter. Instead I stood strong and as composed as I could – even at that moment being aware of my composure and my beloved Hannah at home waiting for me. I felt I could not wail, scream or let out the pain I felt for fear of people thinking I was unfit to look after Hannah. All these years on and whenever I hear that poem it always has me in floods of tears.

The next few months were an absolute blur. Looking back at photos of that time my eyes looked blank and expressionless. It was Hannah that gave me a reason to get up in the mornings and keep going. Without having her and thinking of her I really do not think I could have gone on. I certainly would not have got up out of bed.

My daily routine would involve the care of her and visiting the cemetery. Her smiley face and little pigtails were the only thing that gave me any sense of joy. I could not bear to see dying, wilting or no flowers on Harriet's grave. It was a mission and a mission I kept up for three long years. It just became part of everyday life and I would go and sit and polish the marble and trim around the grave with a pair of scissors to make sure each blade of grass was perfectly even every single day. The seasons would pass, and I would just sit. I look back now and realise I must have been unwell but I had great comfort at the time, great comfort knowing that I may have not had my daughter but I was looking after what I had in the best way I could. The gravestone had become a shrine. I felt like my young and fit body had failed us both and felt tremendous guilt of what I could have done differently.

People say that when someone dies there is a sense of loss, sorry for your loss is a common phrase. I often think what this means. A loss of life? A loss of value in one's own life? Loss of what might have been. Loss as in what? For me, at that period in my life there were periods of complete emptiness and hopelessness and then what I can only describe as a lion roaring in the pit of my stomach. A roar that only I could feel. For me, this loss actually meant a part of me died and even to this day I always feel someone is missing but within my heart.

I had a recurring nightmare. It was the same nightmare every night. I even began to wake myself up halfway through the nightmare as I knew what was going to happen next. I would take a walk downstairs, make a *drink to try and wake myself fully. As soon as closed my eyes the nightmare would start again where it left off. I would always wake again, sit up and let out a silent scream even in my darkest recurring nightmare I was aware I could not scream for real and wake my Hannah. Eventually after six months or so I gave in and visited my doctor. I was almost embarrassed to admit what was happening, worried they may think I was crazy. The doctor explained I had post-traumatic stress disorder and reassured me I was not crazy, just that I had been through a terrible trauma and this was my body's way of releasing stress. They put me in contact with SANDS which is the still born and neonatal death charity who provided me with a weekly counsellor.*

I thought about the doctor's words over and over "terrible trauma" although reassuring I wanted to scream "terrible trauma? who expects their child to die before them? This is not supposed to happen" Even the word terrible trauma did not provide any sort of comfort or justice to my pain. I can't remember if anyone said this to me or whether I came to my own conclusion but I thought to myself daily, if I can get through this and come out the other side I will never feel pain like it again, nothing will come close, and nothing ever has.

Another Physical symptom I had was that I had stopped ovulating. The doctor explained it was due to the shock. Eighteen months later I was prescribed an ovary stimulating drug and became pregnant almost straight away. I was happy but very scared. Petrified in fact.

I was provided with a machine in the house at twenty weeks pregnant which was strapped to my ever-growing bump to record my baby's heartbeat which was then sent directly to the hospital for analysis. I had to do this for the following twenty weeks, four times a day.

My baby was due in January, but the machine picked up a slight decrease in her heartbeat. I was rigid with fear and sadness. I am not at all a religious person but I would get down on my knees and pray. It was agreed I would be induced. I returned to the same hospital. On the 31st of December 2000, Emily was born. She came out screaming. That first scream, I will never forget. The hairs stood up all over my body. She made it. We made it. She was absolutely beautiful. I savoured every moment of that first scream. That was the first moment I felt hope in a very long time and gave a genuine smile for the future in a very long time. I just kept thinking to myself that me and my girl had made it.

Even the midwifes were crying. I was overjoyed. I went on to have a healthy Molly 13 months later. No one has ever replaced Harriet she is still very much with me.

Moving on means acceptance. Something that cannot be changed. 22 years have passed. My daughter is in my heart, I accept that she may not be in anyone else's heart as she is in mine. I accept that when I arrive at the cemetery her grave may need a clean. I visit her grave side twice a year now, once on her birthday when the blossoms are in bloom. Once at Christmas time when the frost is on the ground, knowing there will be no exchange of presents but my gift of love for her and her special place in my heart remains forever.

Acceptance is the greatest gift, one and only one can give to one's self. Moving on and acceptance with my life and the memories that I have, have become more and more integral to defining the person that I have now become. I am now at peace. Grief, I have learned is really just love. It is a deep love that I wanted to give but could not. It was a churning in my stomach, still tears in my eyes or that lump in my throat. It was just my love with no place to go.

I have been blessed with three beautiful daughters, who I love more than anything in this world. It has always felt to me that I only have ever had three quarters of a whole but the missing piece is firmly in my heart.

Always in my heart and never forgotten. Harriet Evans 03.05.1998. Natasha Hamilton-Ash.

Loss of a son

A Mum courageous enough to share her emotional and poignant experience of losing her son.

My darling boy Ben took his own life at age 25, in 2012, whilst he was having treatment for his mental ill health in the local hospital Mental Health unit. They were found to be at fault by the Coroner's inquest after his death as it should not have been possible for him hang himself from the shower rail as he did - what was installed was meant to be unable to bear weight and therefore collapse should suicide be attempted in this manner. It didn't.

When the police knocked on our door just after midnight on the night it happened our world fell apart - and I don't think I have the words to describe the sensation within my body. Ben was at the hospital at his own request, he needed and wanted their help, we had taken him there thinking we were doing the best for him, getting him the help he so desperately needed, how could this possibly happen?

I remember only that I was numb with the shock, initially unable to move except to rock mindlessly to and fro, my arms wrapped around my ribcage as I was in so much pain inside - everything felt as if it was bleeding, breaking, splintering leaving small shards of broken pieces - stabbing me with agonising pain at every thought or movement whilst in my head all I could hear was "I don't know what to do. I don't know what to do, I don't know what to do" - a screaming monotone that wouldn't go away. I know we returned to bed at some point - but I lay staring at the skylight willing this agony to be a nightmare and I would wake and it would be gone. It wasn't.

Over the years since I lost my son - I have discovered that this "club" I was now a member of - The Bereaved Parents Society I call it in my head - is a huge one. In my own family I am the third generation to lose my son, My mum lost her only son - as a baby, My granny lost both her sons, one at 17mnths and one at 21, in my husband's family his nana lost a son, his mother lost one of her sons, and both his sisters have lost a child, one a son & one twin daughters as babes a few months old. So in my immediate family between us we have lost 9 sons/daughters and siblings. Amongst my immediate circle of friends we have also lost 8 sons between us. We are 12 adults to whom this devasting loss has occurred - and I haven't counted stillbirths.

I am sorry I have digressed I think - but doing this for your book made me think about just how many people I know in this club I didn't ever wish to belong to.

Grief I feel for my son doesn't ever go away - I have learned to live with the hole in my heart - some days it is a very tiny hole - some days it so huge I fall right inside and cannot find my way out again - but I am very good a pretending all is ok these days and so I get by. I have my own strategies in place, and there is much more I could write........ Respecting this Mum's wishes. Anon.

Loss of a sister

Heart-felt words from Joanne on the loss of her beloved only sister, Lynda.

I do have some thoughts, I feel quite selfish thoughts but genuine all the same, I feel that when you lose a sibling all the focus goes to the parents (rightly so, no parent should ever have to deal with losing a child) but what about siblings?

As a younger sister I spent my whole life with my sister, from the day I was born she was there, and throughout life, having my children she was with me, thro relationships thro illness, she was always with me, now she gone and I'm left empty, I don't have my sidekick anymore, I don't have that one person who I wholeheartedly could rely on no matter what, and I feel that people don't understand that I am alone and lonely, I want to scream that I'm not OK, but of course I can't do that, I think what I'm saying is spare a thought for the siblings that are left behind, especially if there was only the 2 of them.

(Ohh I didn't expect all that. Wow!)

I could of rabble on forever there, I should start memoirs xx

I think all the raw feelings and emotions from different people will help others understand that what we feel is normal and credited, and we are entitled to the stages of grief that we all go through, I think what your doing is great and can't wait to buy it xx

You can easily go back to a stage that you've already experienced, that's weird, I find it's normally the angry stage, and anger with myself, because I've overthought something that happened years ago and could've handled it differently with Lynda, xx. Joanne Mallinson.

Loss of a father to suicide

This is an emotional heart-felt message from a son, Colin on the loss of his father to suicide (including very much appreciated words of support for me too).

Hi Patricia, I greatly admire how you are continuing to respond so responsibly and positively to your son Bruce's tragic death. I lost my father to suicide when I was three and have only the vaguest of memories of him. However, in my 20's I went to a Christian conference where opportunity was given to forgive if we had ought to forgive. So I nonchalantly mentioned my father. I wasn't ready for the gut wrenching torrent of tears that ensued. I felt totally bereft. At the end someone hugged me and prayed with me, but I left with my brokenness. I had never realised what I was carrying. I felt your book you kindly sent me on 7 attributes for success, while it was achieved through your professional expertise, it also was motivated by a desire to reach out to those facing a predicament like Bruce did. I respect such endeavour. Now you crown it with your latest contribution. May it bring comfort, healing and even closure to those like yourself and indeed to you, foremost. If you can receive it my prayer for you as a living person is perhaps paradoxically Rest in Peace.

Wow!!! I would be Honoured [to be included in this book]*!!! (I wasn't expecting that!) if you feel it would be of value, by all means. Now, please spare my indulgence, I don't think I've ever had my name in print in a book and I would be delighted (tickled pink!!!! - excuse me...) if my name was mentioned!*

If we didn't love, life would be a piece of cake! But a broken heart means you've loved xx

Yes.. Feeling blessed. (once again Patricia has facilitated beauty from Ashes - personally for me, too!!) PS. I said 'feeling blessed' merely as a turn of phrase. I put my phone down and walked into the kitchen when I suddenly felt as though I covered in a soft blanket.... That's my Jesus!!!

Colin Goater.

Loss of a Dad

A beautifully written heartfelt poem from Danielle on the recent loss of her Dad, Alex.

The loss of my dad Alex:

It's still early days for us,
you just left us behind,
I can still see your face,
it's fresh in my mind,
Sometimes I wish I could hit the button,
And go back, just press rewind,
But I can't take this pain again,
it's like no other kind...
Your love remains within us
And our tears continue to rush
Yet your voice fades out of mind
Why is it starting to hush?
You fought so hard and made us proud,
You left us in no rush
It was hard for you to leave us as
You knew our hearts would crush...
But it's still early days for us,
You just left us behind,
I hope one day to see again
As without you, I feel blind.

Danielle McGregor.

Loss of Bruce: a true mate and friend

Shortly after the celebration of Bruce's life I received this moving tribute from Bruce's friend Dez:

Your farewell celebration of life service was so beautiful Bruce and I am so very pleased and honoured to have been there to hug your mother, family and friends in both tears and joy and with pride to have known and know you even more through the stories of your life told today to the sounds of the kilt wearing piper on a perfect warm sun glowing Glasgow day as today xxx. You are loved and missed with love. Life is eternal, Love is immortal and death is only a horizon and a horizon is nothing except the limit of our sight – to The Bruce. Dez Clarke

Later Dez shared with me his story of the impact that Bruce had on his and the lives of others as well as his experience on losing loved ones:

Love and prayers and how Bruce impacted his and other's lives from Dez

My Love & Prayers to you Pat & Family x

Bruce has made an immortal mark in our lives & on our worlds x

He to me was so much fun & an intellectually stimulating long time hard working team member with us ALL in the NottingHill Restaurant "The Westbourne" & "Alistair Little" in London!

I as his manager then & during our working years he became loved by our clientele, great friends to All of us, Me & Especially our other Mgr - 'Wood Davis' whom he was long time House & BMX Bike Buddies with too x haaaa haaaa funny 30yr olds peddling home pissed together haaaa haaaa

Then when I married my long time American GF whom Bruce got to know too when she was in London with me & I eventually moved to live in LA, Bruce kept in contact still & Very Soon after made the Massive Journey to visit Me!!!

I was so touched by the effort & he stayed as our house guest x In coming to America as he did in London!!!!

He instantly was out on the LA & Hollywood scene moving & shaking as you should there, sorting out all sorts of stuff, we wouldn't see him for days even.

Before I knew it he'd scored a room in an apartment & jobs & all the big parties, chicks melted at his accent & looks!!! then ended up staying must've been a Year!!!!!

Bruce was so smart & talented having such a personality, such wide knowledge & many interests, sooo many skills that just about everything he put his mind to he mastered & made it his own!!!!!

He had such charm & infectious personality that he made himself known with everybody in town in no time & began working in Hollywood as a Photographic Assistant, very successfully in fact that when was leaving back for blighty he then took all that he had done in America home with him to Scotland & Created his Own Business in Photography! a Studio & began his artistic & commercial campaigns!!!!

This is 'The Bruce' as we called him!!!!! so of course he did!!!!

We watched his work online & I particularly, knowing him as I did was sooo very pleased for & sooo proud of him xxx

I came back to London not long ago after Many yrs & when last we spoke he was gonna come down to visit when I'd got my place sorted, we would hangout & catch up x Bruce & I had Fun but also 'talked'!

I admittedly suffer bouts of depression which as friends Bruce & I would talk about both our dips in to darkness.....

My Mom at 54 suffered & committed suicide as I arrived back in London & my partner had suffered as I did after the death of our baby son........

I was so grateful for our conversations about how this affected us... Bright & bubbly in everything we do outside with everyone, but when alone sometimes ....It's a dark, quiet & lonely room with no windows or light switch, we who suffer with it for days, weeks & years at a time so often don't even realize we've walked into this room, the door slowly closes behind us & locks! before we know it we are locked in with no key, windows, no matches, candle, not able to find even a light switch? But we see many things that could harm us and want to end the misery & loneliness that keeps trapping us in a glass room with no light!!!!!!

Then for as long as it takes we have to find sooo much strength to fight, to kick the door off its hinges & desperately burst back out in to life but quietly still not causing a fuss.......! Unable or Ashamed to tell anyone how upset, lost & weak we have been, that taking so much time to get back out not telling even where we have been????

Last chat Bruce & I ended our talk & decided about a visit either up to him in Scotland to show me around as I'd never been or down to me in London .....Not long after & at the end of May BH Weekend last year .... I got the Tragic & Devastating News of his suicide ....

"I'm heartbroken My Friend. I Miss our Chats, Our Crazy Pa Yes.. Feeling blessed. (once again Patricia has facilitated beauty from Ashes - personally for me, too!!)

Our Argumentative & very Heated Discussions!!! & Sharing our Feelings about Everything in Life & our Private & Difficult Mind Struggles x Thank you x

I soooo Miss your wild stories of your UK & international, Insane Adventures, Escapades, All in part Usually coz of your Womanizing & Trouble Making???? & Most I miss the Laughter You Caused & Created as You Energized Every Space You Entered into with Just Your Presence!

You are so Sadly missed Bruce my friend xxx

I'm not at all ashamed to say I'm crying while writing this, I'm glad I have the emotional engagement with life & feelings I feel so strongly about this & not even speaking to you in person mate but to you & just out there so Your Family Mom Pat, Dad, Brother & Sisters, Nephews & Nieces & friends in Scotland & everywhere all those who Love You or Know You or may not even, just really know the impact you made Mate x

You Handsome, Hilarious, Brilliant, Renaissance Man! Who Lived Life to the Max!!!

We, the left behind, should take note of your example & do the same xxx

Mayday Weekend for the rest of My Life will be a Celebration Dedicated to You my Missed Mate! & All whom I'm with wherever I am in the world will hear of & know my special stories of - "The Bruuuuuce"

"I miss you, but thinking of you only makes Me Smile always" (Just B4 that moment of sadness)...

Say hi to my Mom, My Son & My Ancestors plz mate, Be with all your loved ones passed b4 & Ancestors too x

I should say RiP ....? But really I'd rather think you are still as you were & probably are even now forever having fun so keep doing what you do!!!!!!!

With fondest memories always Bruce x *Dez Clarke.*

COPING TIPS AND EXERCISES

Controlling relationships

I think it worthwhile to talk about the impact of a controlling relationship (and the fact that I did repeat the pattern!) as I am sure some of you will understand and have even experienced this type of relationship.

It has taken me until now to fully understand the impact of a controlling relationship, not just on me, but my children and especially Bruce who found it impossible to cope with and forgive.

Sociopathic and narcissistic behaviour

I have made reference to individuals who may be classed as sociopaths and narcissists. They only care about themselves and expect others, no demand that others 'jump' to their needs which is how some fathers expect their partner and children to do. Bruce knew this and now his siblings are beginning to realise it too. I have talked with others in similar situations and it saddens me to hear the words, '*...he did nothing for us, was never there when we needed him...it would have been better if he had never been in our lives*'.

Despite being confronted with such behaviour such individuals are oblivious to it or, choose to ignore it and continue with their behaviour.

This is a brief overview of my thoughts but hopefully it gives you some idea of how subtle these individuals are and more often than not if there are any problems you are told by them and start to believe that they are 'your fault'. Of course, a psychological diagnosis should be carried out to identify these traits.

When I look back on my life I remember from very early on in my marriage I had to tread carefully around my husband. I recall the general response was, 'it's not me, it's you...'

Having studied psychology I realise that many difficult people are not aware of their behaviour and respond in many different ways, from criticism, silence or even covert aggression.

When dealing with difficult behaviour some individuals will not admit to being wrong. They are unwilling to compromise and can often be vengeful. Such individuals can cause hurt and chaos without leaving any visible scars.

There is much psychological research on behaviour but one book by Simon (2011)[41] resonated with me.

> *Tip: if you find yourself in a toxic relationship or feel that it is too much to bear, I recommend seeking professional advice to help you take good care of yourself and avoid falling into the same type of relationship later on.*

When I am asked why I did not leave earlier, even before Bruce's fateful words, 'Mummy we must leave....' I found it difficult to answer. However, when I look at psychology research on the topic it was of some comfort to understand that I was 'almost under a spell' as narcissistic individuals can be very skilled at getting you to help them out, even take responsibility for their errors or insults. They can also make you feel special and I recall that my ex-husband did buy me clothes and material things. However, some trips abroad were without the children which saddened me as I wanted them there, knowing that they would have enjoyed the adventure. I remember Bruce telling me that when he was young he didn't like me going away.

Coping exercises

Before moving on to the actual exercises I think it is important to understand how you can make these as effective as possible. This is by using a technique called systematic repetition.

Systematic repetition

Systematic repetition is vital to the effectiveness of my techniques and exercises. When you use the techniques regularly they will help your healing and you will feel less anxious and stressed.

Systematic repetition is all about creating good habits. If you are to succeed in improving your overall well-being you need to have tools at your fingertips, but more importantly for these to be effective the only way is for them to become good habits.

To understand how to form good habits, just take a moment to think about any bad habits you have. If you have none then you are one of the lucky few.

It is easy to create a bad habit. All I want you to do is find a way of making the formation of good habits as easy!

When you have experienced a traumatic, tragic event you will feel emotional pain. It can be so heavy that you might find that 'weight' too much to bear. There are ways of lightening the weight and this is where my techniques come in.

---

[41]   Simon, G.K. (2011) *In Sheep's Clothing: Understanding and Dealing with Manipulative People:* Tantor Media, Incorporated

My ABC techniques are particularly good as they are simple and easy to use but very effective as they are proven psychological techniques.

It is notorious how powerful is the force of habit. Charles Darwin[42].

Creating good habits through systematic repetition is a vast topic and the information here is not exhaustive. There are psychological articles[43] on the subject and many references on the worldwide web. As you can see from Darwin's quote the force of habit is powerful.

If you have bad habits, as, like me, I am sure you do, it can be easy to focus on them. I want you to form good habits and repeat them so eventually these might or will remove your bad habits.

We are what we repeatedly do. Excellence, then, is not an act, but a habit. Aristotle

Habits

Take a moment to think about some of your habits. It helps if you can write them down in the space below.

_____

_____

_____

Don't worry if you have written bad and good habits but by writing them down you can look back later and see how well you have done. Hopefully you will have stopped, removed or even avoided the bad habits by using my techniques.

Now ask yourself why you have these habits. The answer is simple: because you have repeated them. An easy example to understand is smoking or eating unhealthily.

When you are experiencing emotional pain it can be comforting to turn to a bad habit, like smoking, drinking alcohol or eating unhealthy foods. In the long term this will impact on your overall health, both mental and physical.

I know from feedback that many of you start with good intentions of using my techniques but then after a short while you give up (you may read them but don't even really start using them)

It is not what you read about my techniques but how you act that makes the difference in your life

---

[42]   *Defining Habits,* Charles Darwin, The Expression of Emotion in Man and Animals (21)

[43]   *Habits: A Repeat Performance*, Neal, David T, Wood, Wendy and Quinn, Jeffrey M. *Journal of Association for Psychological Science,* Vol 15, Issue 4, pages 198-202 *Defining Habits, Dickens and the Psychology of Repetition,* Vrettos, Athena, *Victorian Studies,* Vol 31, 2000

It is important not to get anxious about your habits. You are not alone. I have bad habits too. After all, we are human!

The key is to become aware of them, particularly your bad habits. Once you know what they are you can do something about them.

You have a choice—you can choose to continue repeating your bad habits or you can learn to form new good ones.

A simple way of thinking about repetition is to reflect on something you learned by repeating. I know mine is learning arithmetic tables. I remember repeating 2×2 is 4 and so on. I have never forgotten this. I know that the things I remember best are those I learned through repetition. Equally, repetition applies to forming your new habits.

Crucial to the healing process is to be aware of increasing your bad habits. Your loss has left you empty and in pain. It is easy to isolate yourself and just sit and watch television, smoke or drink too much to dull your pain. You will want to escape from the pain. Your bad habits will not just be physical but mental and emotional too. Whether they are physical, mental or emotional, the process to heal is the same. Using my ABC techniques will help but you must use them regularly.

Past conditioning

One of the reasons you have habits—bad and good—are because you have been conditioned in the past to think, act and behave in certain ways. You need to challenge how you have been conditioned and change your beliefs and attitudes to be more positive. Doing this will help the healing process.

If you have been conditioned as a child to think, act and behave in a negative way then this will continue into adulthood. As a child you did not have the opportunity to choose your beliefs. When you are young you agree with the information given to you by others. You may rebel against these beliefs but when you are young you are not strong enough usually to win the rebellion! However, as an adult you can think for yourself and make choices. After any tragic situation you might want to wallow in negativity for the rest of your life. Yes, you need to grieve but you also need to move forward. I know my son Bruce would want me to do that.

You may reach out to others and that is OK, whether that be friends, family, support groups, professionals but only *you* can make the decision to move forward as positively as possible.

Just a thought?

If you are someone (and I have known some) who has reached out to a counsellor or medical professional but continue to do so for many years ask yourself if you are using the counsellor or professional as a crutch or are you hoping they will take away your pain?

This is understandable but you must remember that only *you* can make the decision to take action to heal and move forward.

Taking action can be very daunting as part of you might want to 'keep' your pain. I know sometimes I have felt like this, probably in the hope that somehow it will bring my son back to me. Of course, this is impossible but as soon as you start to laugh or feel better you can or might feel as if you are dishonouring your loved one. All these feelings are natural and understandable. But do you really want to live that way; grieving forever?

I repeat, only *you* can change but I am certain that those around you would want you to live life to the fullest and your loved one would also want you to do this in memory of them.

> *You affect your subconscious mind by verbal repetition.* D.H. Lawrence

It is important to also understand what creates effective repetition to change a habit. There is much research on 'learning' and how to form new habits and this research has found that to form new habits the repetition process varies between 21 and 30 days. I recommend that you repeat my techniques for at least 30 days for them to become your new habit.

> *Any idea, plan or purpose may be placed in the mind through repetition of thought.* Napoleon Hill

From personal experience I know that if I want to use my techniques to help me heal, I repeat them for 30 days (day and night). The 30-day period means that you practice them regularly for 20 days but if you miss even one day, you need to start the 30-day period again!

This may sound tedious but it is the reason I developed my ABC techniques as they are short, simple and easy to use, yet effective.

I know the above may feel like information overload, but I believe it is important to understand why you are doing something. There is more information on relaxation and other techniques in my *7 Attributes for Success* book as well as on the internet.

> *Thoughts become actions, actions create habits and habits build character.* Anon

> *If you lack courage to start, you have already finished* Anon

So where do you start? My ABC techniques.

When you are grieving, habits that are addictions can create dependency, whether on substances, activities or relationships and these are harmful to you and those around you.

A word of warning about forming a new habit: you may be met with negative comments and attitudes from others, even from close family and friends. They may expect you to always be sad, even disapprove if you laugh. This is because many people do not understand and may not like the change in you even where the change is positive for you.

As you move through the healing process and become more positive about moving forward you may find yourself feeling ashamed or guilty. This can make you give up your new habit and revert to your old habits. You must not feel this about yourself. I am certain your loved one would not want you to feel this way. However, having these feelings helps you to understand that habits have a strong hold on your behaviour.

Habits exercise

When you suffer the loss of a loved one or a tragedy you will experience emotional pain and you might be focusing too much on your bad habits. Look at the list below of good and bad habits and take a moment to think about what harmful bad habits you might be using (which you think (incorrectly) are helping you through your pain). The list is not exhaustive and you might want to add your own bad and good habits.

Bad habits (physical)	Good habits (physical)
Smoking	Eating healthily
Drinking alcohol	Taking time for yourself
Taking harmful substances	Taking healthy exercise
Getting angry	Doing positive mental exercises
Watching too much television	Making positive plans
Gambling	Clearing clutter, tidying up
Taking sleeping pills	Setting a routine which helps reduce stress
Bulimia	Getting positive support if needed
Anorexia	Asking for help if needed
Aggressive (physical)	Not avoiding your pain
Mental/Emotional bad habits	**Mental/Emotional good habits**
Feeling anxious	Dealing with your emotional pain
Avoiding listening	Positive thinking
Feeling stressed	Valuing yourself
Constant complaining	Being calm
Worrying	Caring for yourself
Arguing	Preventing stress before it becomes a problem
Emotionally aggressive	Respecting yourself and others

Knowing your habits and changing your bad habits to good habits is not a cure. If you are experiencing difficulties with any habits, particularly the serious, harmful ones I recommend that you seek appropriate professional assistance.

Follow these simple steps to help you identify and change your bad habits.

Step 1:   *identify* your habits by making a list of your good and bad habits. Draw two columns, good in one column and bad in the other.

Step 2:   *choose and decide* the first small step to help your healing process by choosing 'one' bad habit which is harmful to you and will delay or stop the healing process. Now decide to stop practising that bad habit.

Step 3:   *write/make a note of this one bad habit* because it helps to write down the one bad habit that you want to stop doing. This reinforces your decision to change your habits.

Step 4:   *write about how this bad habit is harmful to you* Ask yourself whether it is stopping you from moving forward and what are the consequences of continuing to practice this bad habit.

Step 5:   *why continue* Ask yourself why you continue to practice this bad habit. What is preventing you from stopping this bad habit which holds you back from healing?

Step 6:   *take small steps* Pressure and stress will be reduced and even prevented if you take small steps to achieve a goal. Do not set yourself unrealistic difficult goals. Do not beat yourself up if you falter at the first step. Encourage yourself. Praise yourself often when you do succeed.

Step 7:   *write a positive affirmation* You can support yourself by writing down a positive statement, that is, an affirmation, to support you in your progress. For example, it might be 'I move forward more positively...in memory of my loved one'.

Always remember that if you are struggling please seek support from experts, medical professionals, support individuals or groups.

A journey of a thousand miles starts with one small step. Chinese proverb

Having a positive mind is very powerful in helping you move forward after a tragedy and particularly when you are experiencing the weight of emptiness through your loss and pain.

I do a MindBites meditation which is very effective if you want to 'let go' or reduce your emotional pain. I repeat the exercise below.

MindBites meditation: letting go exercise: to help you let go of emotional pain

This MindBites meditation is very effective when you want to let go of emotional pain.

Sit comfortably or lie down....................close your eyes.................listen to my voice..............follow my voice.................Choose something or someone that is hurting or has hurt you (even if you are not sure who or what that is). It must be something over which you have no control. The only control you have is over your own feelings.

The hurt and emotional pain will be felt somewhere in your body—take a moment to think of where this pain is—is it your head, your heart, your stomach, your shoulders, your neck........

Now give this feeling (this hurt) a number from Zero to Ten (zero for no pain or hurt and ten for intense pain or hurt)

Now take three deep breaths in to the count of three 1.......2......3........Hold your breath to the count of three..........1.......2.......3........then slowly exhale to the count of three.............1........2..........3

Take a moment to feel your body, every part of your body inside and out.....imagine you can touch every part of your body inside and out.

Breathe slowly into your body....................feel your body fill with breath.

Exhale slowly...........................feel your breath leave your body.

Now breathe in again slowly and imagine sending positive thoughts and feelings (like a smile) to the part of your body that hurts and say silently to yourself, 'I let it go.....I let it go.

Exhale slowly while still sending positive thoughts and good feelings (like a smile) to every part of your body.

Slowly open your eyes...............silently saying in your head, 'I let it go......I let it go...........Now, note what number you rate the pain, hurt or tension.

The number should be lower as the pain and tension should have eased. This may not happen the first time you do this exercise but continue to do and repeat this exercise and your emotional pain will ease.

I do this exercise every time I need to 'let go' of something or someone. It has helped me cope with the loss of Bruce. I can let my emotional pain go—it reduces—but my love and feelings for Bruce remain as strong as always.

Initially I often rate the pain as and 8 or even a 10. After doing this exercise once or twice the number can be as low as 4. By repeating it I can manage to reduce my emotional pain to a 2 (even a 1).

You can repeat this exercise as often as you need or want, whenever your emotional pain is too heavy or the weight of emptiness is too much to bear. It is very effective when trying to let go of emotional feelings such as those of regret or guilt.

Feedback from others shows that it does work. Please try it. It only takes around three minutes to do.

I now provide some more exercises based on my ABC techniques.

My ABC techniques

A for Affirmations

The first letter 'A' of my core techniques stands for affirmations. This technique is a powerful tool in combating the negative aspects of stress and helping you move forward more positively when you have and are still experiencing emotional pain.

This technique is easy to use but do not be fooled by its simplicity. It is a powerful proven psychological tool if practiced regularly and you will take a giant leap towards a new way of thinking about your loss and it will help in your healing process.

People who have experienced terrible tragedy but appear to cope better or indeed do cope better are those who regularly practice my ABC techniques.

Death is a part of life but suffering the loss of a loved one particularly a child is one of the most devastating that any parent can experience. As a parent you never expect to outlive your children.

I found I needed a technique to get me through each day, each moment. I was so glad I had developed my ABC techniques which originally were to help in times of stress and pressure.

However, I found that they helped to make my pain bearable just following my son's death, but they continue to help me because the pain never really goes away. As I have already said in this book, the weight of the pain changes from moment to moment, day to day but through the techniques you can and do learn to endure.

Through affirmations you learn to reduce and even eliminate negative self-talk.

So how can you do this?

Definition: An affirmation is a positive statement used to re-programme your subconscious. It is a statement when said to yourself, over and over, and with feeling, will influence internal forces and manifest change in your life.[44]

Affirmations change how you think and therefore how you view yourself and everything and everyone around you.

Affirmations can also influence your immune system.[45] Richard Davidson's research found that a positive attitude can keep a person healthy. So, it really seems to be 'mind over matter' even when you have experienced loss of a loved one no matter the circumstances.

---

[44] Emile Coue 19th Century French Professor
[45] *Brain Activity Influences Immune Function*, Richard Davidson, Neuroscientist UW Jan 2003

I make no apologies for talking about some of the humorous moments after the loss of my son. I believe that 'laughter is the best medicine' and that one of the simplest ways of feeling better is laughter.[46] Research has shown that humour can help patients heal.

I do appreciate the work of researchers in many disciplines, but I also believe that if something works for you, sometimes even if there is no scientific explanation, then why not try it and use it. My ABC works for me because I have personally experienced how it has alleviated the weight of emptiness, reduced my emotional pain and is helping me heal so that I can endure every moment of every day.

Scientific studies have shown evidence that mental health can directly impact physical health. For example, high stress increases levels of cortisol, which can lead to a range of physical symptoms including digestive issues, weight gain, headaches, and anxiety. So, with a more positive emotional disposition you can help your healing process. In a World Health Organisation (WHO) Report edited by Herrman et al (2005)[47] the WHO defined health as *a state of complete physical, mental and social well-being and not merely the absence of disease or infirmity* and state that *there is no health without mental health*.

> *I say if it is simple to do, alleviates your emotional pain, helps you to heal, then why not do it.*

Affirmations are short positive statements which are effective if regularly used and follow the guidelines below.

3 Ps Principle

- P for personal: this means that you should use the word 'I' which makes the affirmation personal to you.
- P for positive: this means saying something positive and constructive.
- P for past or present (never future): this means that you think of the statement as though it is something that has happened or is actually happening.

If this is your first time using affirmations then you can use the simple affirmation below.

One simple affirmation following the 3 Ps principle is:

- I feel positive.

When you have experienced the loss of a loved one you will probably not be feeling good and this feeling may still be there when you say an affirmation such as the one above.

However, the whole point of using an affirmation is when you are *not* feeling good. Believe me, it does work.

---

[46] *'Humour'* Melissa B. Wanzer, EdD, Professor of Communication Studies, Canisius College, Buffalo, NY *ScienceDaily (Jan. 26, 2008)*

[47] Report by the World Health Organisation (WHO) (2005), Department of Mental Health and Substance Abuse in collaboration with Victorian Health Foundation (VicHealth) and the University of Melbourne edited by Herrman, *Promoting mental health: concepts, emerging evidence, practice* 31 Dec 2005 ISBN 92 4 156294

Say it. Use it. Repeat it. It does help the healing process.

You do not actually have to believe that it works, you just have to say it (in your head, not out loud) 'with feeling'. You will eventually feel the difference and be more positive about your situation and your healing process.

> *Tip:* repetition is the KEY to the benefits of affirmations. Say the affirmation with feeling and repeat it 2 or 3 times silently in your head.

I recommend that you write your own affirmation on a small card and keep it close by (in your wallet, purse, or briefcase) so that you can refer to as often as you need. Every time you feel your emotional pain become too heavy to bear you can bring the card out and look at your affirmation: read it and repeat it.

If doing this is new to you, say your affirmation as often as you can: say, 10 times every morning and every evening for the next few weeks. Soon it will become second nature to you and your way of thinking changes. This method of change is used in cognitive behavioural therapy (CBT)[48]. The link provides some information from the National Health Service (NHS) UK on cognitive behaviour therapy.

Affirmation examples

These examples are tailored to situations where you have lost a loved one, you are experiencing emotional pain and the weight of emptiness is just too heavy to bear.

Confidence and growth

I am confident.
I am free to cry when I want to or need to.
I choose to endure each moment more positively.

Trust in the healing process

I trust myself to heal and move forward.
I treat each day as a new day.

Taking action

I accept my emotional pain.
I accept

Inner strength and courage

I have courage.
I handle my healing positively.
I take responsibility for my healing.

---

[48]   Cognitive Behavioural Therapy: https://www.nhs.uk/conditions/cognitive-behavioural-therapy-cbt/

Creating happiness

I make a positive difference to those around me.
I turn challenges into positive opportunities for myself and others around me.

Sharing and giving

I share and know that it helps others heal.

B for Breathing

Now you may be wondering why my 'B' is for breathing; after all breathing is fundamental to everyday life. So, breathing is really easy, right? It's something you do all the time without thinking about it? You have been breathing ever since you entered this world so why are you suddenly supposed to 'learn' a new way to breathe?

Well here is some news for you. You may not be breathing as effectively as you could. Many people do not take a deep breath; instead puffing up their upper chest when breathing. So, you need to know how to breathe more effectively.

Many of you will do shallow breathing. This is breathing from the upper part of the chest. This is not very effective as it uses up energy rather than giving you energy. When you use effective breathing you will increase your energy and you will feel better in both body and mind. Effective breathing ensures that enough oxygen is flowing to the muscles you are using and helps prevent unnecessary tension. This is particularly important when you have or are experiencing emotional pain. Effective breathing will help alleviate the weight of emptiness—I know because I use this breathing style and it does work.

If you do Pilates or yoga or have trained in drama, singing or acting you may have been taught effective breathing techniques. Pilates is a type of exercise and physical movement that is designed to stretch, strengthen and balance your body. It involves practice of specific exercises together with focused breathing patterns. Pilates[49] is used as a fitness exercise and in sports training and physical rehabilitation of many kinds. However, do not worry if you are not trained as a singer or actor and do not do yoga or Pilates: you can learn effective breathing and it will help reduce the heavy weight of your emotional pain. Read and try some of the exercises below.

Effective breathing exercise

My effective breathing exercise is simple and easy to use. It takes only a matter of minutes to do and is very helpful in calming and relaxing you. I call this my effective breathing exercise. Take a deep breath in through your nose to the count of three, 1....2....3, and hold your breath for the count of three, 1.....2.....3, and then exhale for the count of three, 1....2....3. You can repeat this once more allowing your breathing to slow down. Pay attention to how your breathing feels as you take the breath down into

---

49   Joseph Hubertus Pilates (1883-1967) (New York) *Inventor and promoter of Pilates method of physical fitness*

your body. When you focus on your breathing you will feel calm and relaxed. You will notice your mind calming and begin to feel relaxed.

I have a MindBites[50] meditation video and audio on how to breathe effectively. Why not try it?

The benefits of my effective breathing exercise include helping you to:

- Reduce anxiety and stress
- Be relaxed and calm
- Manage your emotional pain (particularly at times when it feels too much to bear)
- Increase your creativity
- Meditate
- Improve your overall health and wellbeing and much more.

Effective breathing is particularly helpful in times of stress and related illnesses. I am interested the research on breathing which shows that lack of sufficient oxygen going to the cells of the brain can turn on your sympathetic nervous system—your 'fight or flight' response—and make you tense, anxious, irritable and even depressed. Therefore, if you want to avoid this please try to breathe effectively.

If you watch television programmes on singing, the successful candidates may be offered voice coaching. Such coaching provides techniques for breathing because if they train the individual to breathe correctly then they will naturally know how to sing. Of course, it does not mean that they will necessarily sing in tune or win as there are many other factors involved but effective breathing is key.[51]

I was fortunate when young to be sent to elocution and drama. I was trained in breathing techniques which helped with voice production. I did not realise then that these techniques would help me cope with my emotional pain when I lost Bruce to suicide. As I referred to earlier, a friend told me that I cope with my grief well. Of course, they know me well and know that this coping mechanism is for the outside world. I still cry, sometimes (often) uncontrollably, but in private. This is a very necessary release because I know that if I held back it would cause me even more pain and damage my physical and mental health.

There are certain circumstances when you need to maintain composure especially in 'public' situations such as funerals, weddings and other emotional occasions. Such occasions can become even more emotional when you have a lost a loved one. At such times I turn to my calm breathing technique and my 'red door/blue door' technique.

> *Remember: it is unhealthy to withhold your emotions such as crying but with my breathing exercises you can release your emotions in your own time and in your own 'safe' place.*

---

[50]   MindBites – how to breathe effectively available on www.mindcircles.co.uk or www.stepsforsuccess.co.uk
[51]   Framingham study at the National Institute of Health Database www.ncbi.nlm.nik.gov/PubMed/

Calm breathing exercise

My calm breathing exercise is helpful if you feel tears and emotions rising to the surface especially at moments when you want or need to remain calm and composed. For this exercise you take a deep breath in through your mouth and then push your breath out through your nose. Any time I feel tears or emotion rising I use this calm breathing exercise. It is simple, quick and very effective.

Testimonial: A Director of a company had to give a public announcement about the unexpected closure of his plant was concerned about letting his emotions overwhelm him. He is a very caring man. He told me that he could not have spoken in public if he had not used my ABC core techniques, particularly the 'calm' breathing which he used before and (subtly) during the actual announcement. He said it was simple, easy to do and no-one noticed.

In my MindBites meditative videos and audios I have one called 'How to breathe effectively' that shows you how to breathe effectively. Effective breathing helps you to:

- Be energised
- Be calm
- Be relaxed

Like affirmations, my breathing exercises are simple but extremely effective.

Focus breathing exercise

This breathing exercise helps you to relieve anxiety, tension and stress which is particularly helpful when you are experiencing emotional pain after the loss of a loved one.

In this exercise you breathe from the lower part of your lungs to the top part (as in deep breathing) through your nose (remember it is important to breathe through your nose). Keep your mouth closed and then push your breath out with a deep sigh. This empties the lungs of old, stale air. This creates 'space' to enable you to fill up your lungs with new 'clean' air (or as clean as it can be in this polluted world!). Do this three or four times. Do not worry if find this difficult, it will become easier with practice.

Relaxation breathing

This is an excellent breathing exercise to help you relax and be calm. It can also help if you are having difficulty sleeping which is very understandable if you have suffered the loss of a loved one. It is best if you are sitting comfortably or lying down.

Read the exercise below until you are ready to do it. Then try it with your eyes open and then once familiar with it, close your eyes and do it again.

Body part	Approx. time	Procedure for the exercise
Toes	5 secs	Feel and focus on your toes by holding them tightly, then release and relax them, wiggling your toes
Ankles	5 secs	Pull your toes towards your head, focus on your ankles, hold for 5 seconds and then relax
Legs	9 secs	Stretch your legs stiffly, focus on them. Begin at the calf for 3 seconds then relax, then the knees for 3 seconds then relax, then the thighs for 3 seconds then relax.
Arms	10 secs	Stretch your arms straight in front, pull hands and fingers together. Hold for 10 seconds and then relax.
Shoulders	12 secs	Pull your shoulders up towards your ears. Hold for 4 seconds and then relax slowly, breathing out as you relax. Repeat twice.
Face	12 secs	Balance your head squarely on your shoulders to release any tension in the neck area. Screw your face up tightly. Hold for 12 seconds, then relax. Unclench your teeth and open your mouth slightly, relaxing it. Repeat twice.
Eyes	5 secs	Lightly close your eyes, then tightly shut them, then relax the eyelids. This is the finishing part of the exercise.

Do not do this exercise if you are driving or operating machinery. It is intended for when you have a quiet moment to yourself.

I find this exercise helps when I feel the weight of emptiness becoming too heavy to bear. Doing this exercise gives me 'time out' when I only focus on what I am doing. Of course, the above exercise takes time so remember if you need a quick 'fix' then just take three deep breaths.

There are many different types of breathing exercises and you can find them by searching the internet. However, the purpose of the above breathing exercises is to help you in times of extreme emotional distress. Since losing my son I use them often. If you regularly practice my breathing exercises, then you too will have them to hand when you want or need them.

If even my breathing exercises become too much to think about in times of need then just remember this tip.

> *Remember: if your emotional pain is becoming too much to bear and the weight of emptiness is just too heavy then take three deep breaths. This will calm you down.*

C for creative imagery

I am enough of an artist to draw freely upon my imagination. Imagination is more important than knowledge. Knowledge is limited. Imagination encircles the world.
Albert Einstein

The 'C' of my ABC core techniques is just as important as the others for helping you cope with your emotional pain. Creative imagery is sometimes known as visualisation.

I have developed a MindBites[52] video on how to visualise. I did this because from my experience speaking with many people over the years I realised that many people found visualisations difficult to do. From feedback I discovered that this was because they are called visualisations which people tended to think of as 'seeing'. When I explained it was about using your imagination it became clearer. I further explained that it is all about imagining and using the one or more of your five senses that you find easiest to use when imagining, whether that is see, hear, touch, smell, or taste.

Like me, Bruce was always good at imagining. Indeed, again like me, he probably had an over-active imagination. Rather than call it visualising or imagining I wanted something that linked in with my affirmations (A), my breathing (B), so I decided that I would call it creative imagery and it became my 'C' of my ABC.

Creative imagery examples

A hearing example: if you use your hearing, the scenario for the creative imagery of the seaside might be to close your eyes, think of yourself at the seaside and hear the sea lapping on the sand or the birds singing above or the wind whistling in the grass.

A sense of smell example: for those who use their sense of smell, the scenario would be to smell the sea air, smell the fresh grass, smell the salty air and so on. Hopefully, you now 'get the picture or should I say, message'.

Of course another problem with using your imagination is that as a child you probably had no problem in using your imagination but as you grew up you were probably told 'be in the real world' or 'not to daydream'.

> *Remember: You can achieve great things through imagination. Champion athletes do!*

---

[52]   MindBites video how to visualise

The difficulty with imagination when you are experiencing emotional pain is that it can surface memories which can create more pain. However, when you lose a loved one it is your positive memories that keep you going. I referred earlier to feelings of guilt when you lose someone as you wonder if you could have done more or done something differently. When I talk about my creative imagery exercise, I want you to think of all the beautiful memories. Nothing will bring your loved one back but I am certain they would not want you to be sad forever.

Creative imagery is also about the power of the mind. The effectiveness of using creative imagery was highlighted in a BBC science television programme. The programme followed the training of a young gymnast, a 14-year old girl, in her dreams of competing in the Olympics. Each time her coach put her through her new double bar exercise she failed to grasp the top bar. Now you would expect that continual practice of the actual routine would be the best way of improving. However, her coach asked her to take time out and use her 'mind' to practice. Amazingly after repeatedly imagining herself doing the new routine perfectly she was able to actually do it perfectly. This is how effective creative imagery was used in the real world.

Other types of mental training include hypnotherapy and Neuro Linguistic Programming (NLP).

You do not necessarily need to learn these methods. You can learn to do creative imagery yourself. If you are struggling with your emotional pain I recommend that you seek professional help. Having a few techniques and exercises that you can use yourself also helps alleviate your emotional pain and creative imagery is one of the most powerful mental training exercises. It is used by top athletes and successful people all over the world. Such people are able to move forward positively no matter the challenges they have faced.

Whether you know it or not you use your imagination every day, all day. You are using your imagination when you think of your lost loved one. However, without realising it when you start to cry or feel the weight of emptiness too much to bear these are the negative emotions you are imagining and then acting on. What I want you to do is turn those negative imaginations into positive ones. Athletes who experience recurring problems of failure are usually imagining failure, hindering their efforts from the beginning. What the successful ones do is to overcome this way of imagining by changing their mind and thoughts into positive ones.

Some benefits of creative imagery (C) include:

- Reduced and even removal of negative thoughts and negative self-talk
- Reduced nervousness and anxiety
- Increased belief in yourself and your ability to heal
- Increased confidence in yourself that you can move forward positively.

Scientific journals[53] are painting a picture of the impact of visualisation in psychology, education, the arts and literature, sociology and much more. Physicists have begun to study subtle body energies and

---

[53]   Journal of Mental Imagery

their effect on the world outside the body. Philosophers over the years have recognised this energy. The Chinese call it *chi*, the Japanese call it *ki*, the Indians call it *prana*. It is used in therapy all over the world.

I use creative imagery every day. I use it to remember my wonderful son and my beautiful memories. I remember his letter to me and use it to imagine how he would want me to live.

> *The mind is a very powerful tool. Use it always.* Anon.

When you want or need to alleviate your emotional pain you can feel better if you use my 'C' and let your imagination flow. Even letting tears flow while you imagine is good for your body, mind and soul.

I have created MindBites videos and audios on different topics. Here are some of the titles and information which are more relevant to emotional pain experienced on the loss of a loved one. Please use them regularly. They do work. They relax, calm and energise you. More than that, they can help you to find the courage and resilience to face life's challenges and move forward more positively.

MindBites meditations – Creative imagery titles and information

MindBites: How to visualise

Knowing you have lost a loved one, imagine a happy memory. Relax and breathe deeply. Think of this memory for a moment or two. Close your eyes. Say, for example, this event is a holiday that you had together or as a family by the sea. Do you:

- 'hear' the sea (the waves crashing or water lapping)
- 'see' the colour of the waves (blue, green, grey, white surf)
- 'feel' the water (cool, warm, crashing against your legs or lapping against your legs)
- 'smell' the freshness of the sea air (salty, fresh, fishy)
- 'taste' the water (salty sea, salty air on your lips)

or

- hear the silence
- see the beauty
- feel as if you could touch the water
- smell the ferns and the wildflowers
- taste the purity of the air?

You might use more than one of your senses and that is fine. Use whatever works for you. My 'C' can be very effective if you close your eyes while imagining.

I have created my MindBites as short meditations with calming, ambient music to help you relax. I realised that many of the relaxing meditations were too long, certainly for me, so I wanted something that was short but still effective. Of course, they can be played repeatedly when you want or need. Here are some MindBites titles and how they help you.

- The Golden Sphere, to help you feel relaxed, calm and safe.
- A Safe Place, to help you feel safe
- Calm Lake, to help you feel a sense of peace
- Beach and horizon, to help you feel confident
- The Meadow and tree, to help you feel confident and strong
- Floating Clouds, to help you feel calm and at peace
- Golden Sunset, to help you move forward
- Changing Seasons, to help you face change
- The Beach, to help you quietly reflect and feel at peace
- Colours, to help you relax
- Ribbons, to help you let go
- Star breath, to help with addiction

The above titles may change and I continue to add MindBites meditations on other topics.

Stress symptoms and areas affected by stress

When you have suffered a loss or tragedy and are experiencing emotional pain you may experience stress and anxiety. This is natural and understandable.

However, it is important to know and understand the symptoms of stress and anxiety and how it can affect you.

The table of symptoms below is not exhaustive but is intended to provide you with some information.

If you are suffering from stress and anxiety and have feelings of not being able to cope, I recommend that you seek professional support.

Cognitive Symptoms	Emotional Symptoms
• Memory problems	• Moodiness
• Indecisiveness	• Agitation
• Inability to concentrate	• Restlessness
• Trouble thinking clearly	• Short temper
• Poor judgment	• Irritability, impatience
• Seeing only the negative	• Inability to relax
• Anxious or racing thoughts	• Feeling tense and "on edge"
• Constant worrying	• Feeling overwhelmed
• Loss of objectivity	• Sense of loneliness and isolation
• Fearful anticipation	• Depression or general unhappiness

Physical Symptoms	Behavioural Symptoms
• Headaches or backaches • Muscle tension and stiffness • Diarrhoea or constipation • Nausea, dizziness • Insomnia • Chest pain, rapid heartbeat • Weight gain or loss • Skin breakouts (hives, eczema) • Loss of sex drive • Frequent colds	• Eating more or less • Sleeping too much or too little • Isolating yourself from others • Procrastination, neglecting responsibilities • Using alcohol, cigarettes, or drugs to relax • Nervous habits (e.g. nail biting, pacing) • Teeth grinding or jaw clenching • Overdoing activities (e.g. exercising, shopping) • Overreacting to unexpected problems • Picking fights with others

Life events stress scale

The table below is adapted from Holmes-Rahe *Social Readjustment Rating Scale*[54], Journal of Psychosomatic Research, Vol II, 1967.

I provide this table to help you understand the effect of loss of a partner or loved one has on your stress levels.

No.	Event description	Points
Life Event Mean Value		
1	Death of spouse/partner	100
2	Divorce	73
3	Marital Separation from mate	65
4	Detention in jail or other institution	63
5	Death of a close family member/loved one	63
6	Major personal injury or illness	53
7	Marriage	50
8	Being fired at work	47
9	Marital reconciliation with mate	45
10	Retirement from work	45
11	Major change in the health or behaviour of a family member	44
12	Pregnancy	40
13	Sexual Difficulties	39
14	Gaining a new family member (i.e., birth, adoption, older adult moving in, etc)	39
15	Major business readjustment	39
16	Major change in financial state (i.e., a lot worse or better off than usual)	38
17	Death of a close friend	37

---

[54]   Holmes–Rahe (1967) *Social Readjustment Rating Scale* Journal of Psychosomatic Research, Vol II

18	Changing to a different line of work	36
19	Major change in the number of arguments with partner/spouse (i.e., either a lot more or a lot less than usual regarding child rearing, personal habits, etc.)	35
20	Taking on a mortgage (for home, business, etc.)	31
21	Foreclosure on a mortgage or loan	30
22	Major change in responsibilities at work (i.e., promotion, demotion, etc.)	29
23	Son or daughter leaving home (marriage, attending college, joined the forces.)	29
24	In-law troubles	29
25	Outstanding personal achievement	28
26	Spouse beginning or ceasing work outside the home	26
27	Beginning or ceasing formal schooling	26
28	Major change in living condition (new home, refurbishing, deterioration of neighbourhood or home etc.)	25
29	Revision of personal habits (dress manners, associations, quitting smoking)	24
30	Troubles with the boss	23
31	Major changes in working hours or conditions	20
32	Changes in residence	20
33	Changing to a new school	20
34	Major change in usual type and/or amount of recreation	19
35	Major change in church activity (i.e., a lot more or less than usual)	19
36	Major change in social activities (clubs, movies, visiting, etc.)	18
37	Taking on a loan (car, TV, freezer, etc.)	17
38	Major change in sleeping habits (a lot more or a lot less than usual)	16
39	Major change in number of family get-togethers	15
40	Major change in eating habits (a lot more or less food intake, or very different meal hours or surroundings)	15
41	Vacation	13
42	Major holidays	12
43	Minor violations of the law (traffic tickets, jaywalking, disturbing the peace, etc.)	11

A score of at least 300 points raises the odds of being stressed to about 80%, according to the Holmes–Rahe statistical prediction model.

As you can see from the table, loss of a loved one or someone close to you as a huge impact on how you feel and significantly raise the odds of being stressed.

Why not look at the above table and make a note of the points for each life event that you have experienced during the past year. Add these up to find your score.

A score of 150 points or less means a relatively low amount of life change and a low susceptibility to stress-induced health breakdown.

A score of between 150 and 300 points implies about a 50% chance of a major health breakdown in the next two years.

> Recommendation: *No matter your score you should still use my ABC techniques and any exercises you can to help alleviate your emotional pain so that you can move forward as positively as you can.*

Red door/blue door

This exercise may seem ridiculous, but it does work. I have personal experience of using it and I have tried it with many others.

The reason that it works is because you cannot break down and cry or be emotional when you are doing something cognitive. Emotions and cognitions just do not work together.

I nearly forgot my own exercise when I was going into the crematorium. It was my daughter who whispered to me, 'Remember, red door/blue door'. I was so thankful that she reminded me as I was able to speak, without crying or breaking down, about my gorgeous son and pay my respect to and love for him at the celebration of his life.

There are other techniques to use when you want to remain calm and composed but I find this one very easy to use.

You silently say to yourself the words 'red door/blue door'. You can keep repeating these words in your head (even when you are giving a speech or talk). At any moment between words, or when you are 'pacing' yourself when talking you can silently repeat these words.

I spoke to the celebrant as she was very composed and knowing Bruce I wondered how she maintained that composure. She does have a technique but suffice to say I will keep that one to myself!

Another way of thinking about this exercise is to look around and see if you can spot the colour red and blue. As long as you are not thinking about your emotions, it will work.

There is much research on cognition and emotion and the link between them, or whether they are independent of each other or inter-dependent. The above exercise is only my view and as it works for me; I hope it works for others too.

BLOGS – EXCERPTS FROM BEFORE AND AFTER MY LOSS

I am an avid blogger and wrote about many topics, including grief, before Bruce's death. However, after losing him to suicide I continued to write blogs but, I believe that I wrote with more insight into what it is like to experience loss of a loved one. I include three excerpts from my own blogs on my thoughts of my loss. The first blog was written before I lost my son to suicide and the other three were written by me after his death.

The excerpt below is about my thoughts on loss and comes from a blog I wrote (29th August 2013) some 9 months *before* Bruce's death.

Coping with loss

'..............*Losing someone you love .... there is always pain for you, your family and close friends.................when the death is sudden you will find it very difficult to cope as you are overwhelmed and your ability to cope is greatly diminished because you are in a state of shock and stunned by the suddenness of the loss of your loved one. You will suffer extreme feelings of anxiety............be bewildered......................... self-critical and reproach yourself with the what if....................When death is sudden you have had no time to prepare or take in the fact that your world was about to dramatically change.........it has been snatched from you and you have had no time to make changes in yourself or expectations about your life......there is a massive gap between your world with your loved one and the way it will be now. The loss of your loved one takes away any sense or control of your world. Everyone experiences grief and loss in a different way but coping mechanisms can be different when your loss is sudden and unexpected....................Where you have had time to prepare and even been able to try to make sense of it all ....you may have been able to say I love you............your coping mechanism is different...................Where death is sudden and unexpected you are so shocked that you cannot understand what has happened and you will find it difficult to understand the implications of your loss. Although you may intellectually recognise that it has happened you might or will find it difficult to accept that the death happened........................you go over the story of what happened again and again to try to make sense of your loss......................you may or will repeatedly go over the time leading up to the death, searching for clues that could have indicated what was to come.............this is understandable and quite common......................it can make the situation more manageable as it gives you some control over the situation.............. Be warned that problems can arise when you carry out 'reconstructing' if you hold yourself responsible for not perceiving or seeing the clues that may have been there but were imperceptible or even non-existent before the death (remember there may be no way that you could have known). When death is sudden your grief symptoms may tend to go on longer.................... and you will feel physically, mentally and emotionally depleted. Your anxiety and trauma is also increased as you were not able to say your goodbyes and had no opportunity to finish unfinished business with your loved one or were unable to bring a positive close with the person you loved ....you will wish you had just one more moment to tell them you loved them..............you will feel a profound loss of security and confidence in your world.................you learn a tragic life lesson that loved ones can be snatched away without warning................even believing that another loss might happen .... even withdrawing from the world as it has become a frightening and unpredictable place..................... many wonderful people who are positive and strong have told me they turn such tragedy into something meaningful...........and that their loved ones would want it to be so. Remember you can and will survive the pain even though there may be, or will be, times when you don't think it possible, but it is. Do what is right for you...............everyone grieves in different ways and pace.....there is no timeline for healing............ special days will be difficult, decide what you want to do..............expect to have waves of sadness............ feeling overwhelmed is very normal.........feel angry, confused, guilty are common responses to death – you are not going crazy..............go over these feelings until you can let them go...........letting go does not mean forgetting...... take care of yourself............enjoying life is not betraying your loved one.............it is a sign you are beginning to heal.................laughing is part of the healing process. You will never be the same again but you will survive.* Patricia Elliot

This next two excerpts are from my blog (25th June 2014) written a few weeks after my son Bruce committed suicide.

Find your 'why'

This is for you Bruce – I know you did not find your 'why' in this life but am certain you will find it now. This message is for everyone – please find your 'why'.

My oldest son Bruce took his own life on 5 May 2014. This tragedy has affected so many people who have contacted me by phone, email and social media thanking me for my honesty in telling of his death and how. I believe it is important not to hide 'suicide'. Since that terrible day I have discovered that there are many more suicides than we hear about. People may be frightened or ashamed and I no longer want this to be the case. I write this to help raise awareness of suicide and help those left behind.

However instead of talking about the sadness of which there is much – not a day goes by without me wanting to speak with him, hold him, hug him and have our wonderful chats on many topics of which he seemed to have an endless source of information. Bruce used to come to me with lots of psychology tips and techniques for my MindCircles programs or blogs. He was so eager that people would benefit from them yet he could not feel able to practice them himself......

I miss him so and although there is a lot of 'bubbling' (that is crying to those outwith Scotland!!) I try and manage to remember all the funny, quirky things about him.

If only..................

If only I could have cloaked him in confidence and resilience then I would have done so (and I tried) but if nothing else comes out of this tragedy it is to let everyone know that change of any kind including confidence and resilience must come from within. The hardest thing that I have ever had to do was 'speak' to my wonderful son Bruce at the celebration of his life but I was not going to let that day go by without letting him know how much I loved him and how much he was loved by everyone from places all round the world'. Patricia Elliot

When I started writing blogs some 10 years ago I wrote about resilience on a few occasions. A few months after I lost my son I felt compelled to write again about resilience (3rd September 2014). Here is an excerpt.

Resilience – become strong

'......................................there have been many ups and few downs and I have needed my 2nd Attribute resilience in abundance......................... resilience is bouncing back against adversity. This is not easy and some have more than others.

Talking about resilience is difficult for me as I reflect back on Bruce, my gorgeous son who took his own life in May 2014. He was just not able to overcome some adversities despite being such a promoter of my 'tips and tools'. I looked back on situations and people that had upset him and I used to say to him that the best form of revenge is to succeed in the face of it all. He would try and I prayed that he would find that resilience but as soon as anxiety kicked in he would find resilience evaded him. So I know first-hand that being resilient is not easy but ....it is fundamental to achieving inner success and happiness'. Patricia Elliot

Some two years after Bruce's death a good friend and colleague, who had experienced the tragic loss of a loved one, wrote a poignant and emotional blog (26th April 2016) which I published on my website with his permission. Here is an excerpt, quoted with his permission, and I am sure that many will empathise with this.

Fix You

'Sometimes I wish I were a boy again, running home to Mum with trousers torn at the knee and underneath, a skinned knee, bleeding like it will never stop............................ I knew she would fix it; both the trousers and the knee, that overwhelming joy that ran through me because I knew that in a few hours I would have no pain, my trousers would be mended and I would have been forgiven and cared for again and – FIXED.

As I finally walk away from the small grave, with broken heart and a pain that I had not experienced ever before. I wished and wished that I was running home to Mum so that she could fix it... that feeling of knowing, that in a few hours all of it would be fixed, forgiven. Life moving on as if it had never happened. If only............... If only..............

There are times when there are too few words left to heal us, no actions left that can help us, when what we wish for is to be carried, cared and understood, but all those around you have no understanding, how could they..............just impossible. All that is left is the hope that tomorrow will be a more gentle place to land than today.

I read somewhere 'Missing someone gets easier every day because even though it's one day further from the last time you saw each other, it's one day closer to the next time you will.' Of all the times it has been said to me that time is a healer, it was not until I read those few words that I started to believe that time is a healer; I stopped thinking of its negative effect that when said makes you feel guilty because you think time is healing by making you forget. The passing of time is simply watering down the grief, not the memory, the memory stays rock solid, this way, when you meet again, the wilderness in between will matter not. W.T.

LIST OF PHOTOGRAPHS

Description	Page No.
Bruce face – dark blue with light shining	Front
Bruce's photo of building with 'shape' & Bruce's face	Back
Collage of Bruce	iii
Bruce – thoughtful sitting	xv
Three faces of Bruce – (sad, sombre, happy)	2
Some of Bruce's swimming medals	5
Bruce & his brother as cartoon characters: drawn by Bruce	8
Bruce's graduation	10
Bruce's sculptures	12
Bruce's sculpture exhibition leaflet	13
Bruce - various acting roles	19-22
Bruce's fashion photography	26
Bruce's photography various photos of Scotland, Cuba and New York	28-30
Bruce's psychoactive photos	31-32
Bruce's teddy & me	56
Bruce's garden in Denmark	58
Bruce's brother scattering ashes in the Pacific ocean	58
Sunset sky – clouds like 2 people (courtesy of Charlie Francis)	61
Bruce – Happy Mother's Day	143

Index